THE GOONERS
QUIZ BOOK

THE GOONERS
QUIZ BOOK

COMPILED BY
CHRIS COWLIN

APEX PUBLISHING LTD

First published in 2006 by

Apex Publishing Ltd

PO Box 7086, Clacton on Sea, Essex, CO15 5WN, England

www.apexpublishing.co.uk

British Library Cataloguing-in-Publication Data
A catalogue record for this book
is available from the British Library

ISBN 1-904444-77-6
978-1-904444-77-0

Typeset in 10.5pt Chianti BdIt Win95BT

Cover Design: Andrew Macey

Printed and bound in Great Britain

Author's Note:
Please can you contact me: ChrisCowlin@btconnect.com if you find any mistakes/errors in this book as I would like to put them right on any future reprints of this book. I would also like to hear from Arsenal fans who have enjoyed the test!

This book is in no way officially associated with Arsenal Football Club

This book is dedicated to:

my Uncle, Colin - a dedicated Arsenal fan

and

*my Dad, Martin - an Arsenal fan as a boy,
BUT a Spurs fan now!*

FOREWORD

I first set eyes on Highbury in February 1963. I had travelled south from Loughborough College at the request of Billy Wright, an England legend and the manager of Arsenal at the time. That year I became an Arsenal player (as an amateur) and played my first game on that hallowed turf against Nottingham Forest in the October.

This great club has been part of my life ever since my first journey to N5 and so it is both a pleasure and an honour to write this foreword to The Gooners Quiz Book.

I am especially pleased that Chris Cowlin has, once again, selected the Willow Foundation as the charity to benefit from every book sold. I founded the Willow Foundation with my wife Megs in 1999, after our daughter Anna died of cancer just before her 32nd birthday. The Willow Foundation provides 'special days' for seriously ill young adults and we feel privileged that the charity has been nominated as Arsenal's Charity of the Year for the first year at the Emirates Stadium.

I have lived with the Gunners for over 40 years and I can assure the readers of this book that they are in for a treat. Chris has put together a blend of club history, legendary players and memorable occasions. I feel certain that the reader will enjoy the questions from start to finish.

Bob Wilson

INTRODUCTION

I would first of all like to thank Arsenal and footballing legend Bob Wilson for writing the foreword to this book. I am very grateful for his help on this project. I would also like to thank the following people for their comments and support for this book: Tony Adams, Alan Smith, Graham Rix, Brian Talbot, David O'Leary, David Seaman, Frank McLintock, Charlie George and Ian Allinson.

I would personally like to thank Fraser MacKenzie and Martin O'Donnell who are the secretary and chairman of the Arsenal Scotland Supporters Club - they have been great and extremely helpful to me while compiling this book, please take time to view their website, I am sure you will find something of interest: www.arsenalscotland.com I would also like to thank Stuart Haigh for help whilst compiling the book.

I am honoured to donate £1 from each book sale to 'The Willow Foundation Charity'. It is a registered charity - www.willowfoundation.org.uk dedicated to improving the quality of life of seriously ill young adults aged 16 to 40 throughout the UK, by organising and finding a 'Special Day' of their choice. I would like to thank the Chief Executive of The Willow Foundation, David Williams, for his support in creating this book.

I hope you enjoy this book, it was a pleasure compiling it as the club has so much history and success, I am sure whatever section you choose to read first will make you smile and the memories will come flooding back!

Chris Cowlin

Best wishes
Chris Cowlin

DAVID O'LEARY

1.   In what year was David born - 1957, 1958 or 1959?

2.   Which country did David represent at international level?   *Sweden*

3.   When David left Arsenal which club did he join?   *R. Madrid*

4.   How many caps did David win for his country - 62, 64 or 68?

5.   Against which club did David make his Arsenal debut in August 1975?   *Chelsea*

6.   How many League appearances did David make for Arsenal?   *48*

7.   How many League goals did David score for Arsenal in his career?

8.   During Arsenal's championship success in 1990/1991, David made 21 appearances, scoring one goal. Which team was that against?

9.   In which Arsenal Cup Final did David make the starting eleven during May 1993?

10.   Which Yorkshire team did David manage after he finished his playing career with them?

1

THE LEAGUE CUP

11. Which player scored a hat-trick against Leeds United in a 7-0 2nd round win in September 1978?

12. Against which two London sides did Arsenal play during the 1997/1998 season?

13. Which player scored a hat-trick v. Huddersfield Town in a 5-0 2nd round win in September 1993?

14. Sylvain Wiltord scored a hat-trick in a 4-0 win in the 3rd round in November 2001, against who?

15. Which player scored a hat-trick against Plymouth Argyle in a 5-0 2nd round win in October 1989?

16. How many League Cup trophies did Arsenal win under George Graham?

17. Which two players scored five goals between them in a 5-0 2nd round win over Hartlepool United in October 1995?

18. In which year did Arsenal first win the League Cup?

19. Which player scored Arsenal's two goals in their first League Cup Final win?

20. Which goalkeeper played in Arsenal's four League Cup goals in the 1983/1984 season?

IAN WRIGHT

21. In which year was Ian born - 1961, 1962 or 1963?

22. From which club did Arsenal sign Ian in September 1991?

23. How much did George Graham pay for Ian?

24. Ian made 278 starts and nine substitute appearances for Arsenal. How many goals did he score?

25. Ian scored a hat-trick in a 4-1 win at Highbury in September 1996. Which team was it against?

26. In Arsenal's first Premier League season, how many goals did Ian score - 13, 15 or 17?

27. Ian scored a hat-trick against Ipswich Town in April 1995 in a 4-1 win. Who scored the other?

28. Against which club did Ian score his first Arsenal hat-trick in September 1991?

29. How many European Cup Winners' Cup goals did Ian score in the build-up to the 1995 Final?

30. Against which team did Ian play in his last League game for the Gunners?

BRIAN TALBOT

31. In what year was Brian born - 1951, 1952 or 1953?

32. From which club did Arsenal sign Brian in 1979?

33. When Brian left the Gunners which team did he join?

34. For which Midlands club did Brian play during his career?

35. What was Brian's nickname at Highbury?

36. Which manager signed Brian for Arsenal in 1979 for £450,000?

37. How many League goals did Brian score for Arsenal?

38. In the 1979 FA Cup Final Brian scored the first goal in the 3-2 win over Manchester United. Who scored Manchester United's two goals?

39. Which club did Arsenal beat 1-0, with Brian scoring the goal, in the 1980 FA Cup Semi-Final?

40. Brian played in all 42 Division One games during 1981/1982. How many goals did he score?

ARSENAL: THE SUCCESS

All you have to do is match the success with the year that Arsenal achieved it

41.	League Champions, Won 22, Pts 76	2003
42.	FA Cup Winners, 2-0 v. Chelsea	1931
43.	FA Cup Winners, 2-0 v. Huddersfield Town	1994
44.	League Champions, Won 23, Pts 91	1950
45.	League Champions, Won 28, Pts 66	1989
46.	FA Cup Winners, 1-0 v. Southampton	1998
47.	League Cup Winners, 2-1 v. Sheffield Wednesday	2002
48.	FA Cup Winners, 2-0 v. Liverpool	1993
49.	FA Cup Winners, 3-2 v. Manchester United	1930
50.	European Cup Winners' Cup Winners, 1-0 v. Parma	1979

MANAGER: GEORGE GRAHAM

51. How many League titles did Arsenal win under George as manager?

52. Which Cup did Arsenal win in George's first season in charge of Arsenal?

53. George signed for Arsenal from Chelsea in 1966. Which manager signed him?

54. When George signed for Arsenal from Chelsea which player went in the other direction?

55. Which club did George manage between 1982 and 1986?

56. How many Scotland caps did George win?

57. How many FA Cup trophies did Arsenal win under George as manager?

58. At which London club did George end his playing career?

59. Which club did George take over as manager in 1996?

60. How many League goals did George score in his Arsenal career - 59, 69 or 79?

LEAGUE POSITIONS - 1

Match the season with the position that Arsenal finished

61.	2001/2002	Premier League	5th
62.	1999/2000	Premier League	9th
63.	1996/1997	Premier League	1st
64.	1992/1993	Premier League	3rd
65.	1982/1983	Division One	10th
66.	1981/1982	Division One	2nd
67.	1973/1974	Division One	10th
68.	1961/1962	Division One	3rd
69.	1954/1955	Division One	10th
70.	1951/1952	Division One	10th

1998/1999

71. Who did Arsenal beat 2-1 at Highbury on the opening day of the season?

72. Arsenal's highest win this season was 6-1. Which team was it against?

73. At which position did Arsenal finish in the Premier League?

74. Which player finished as highest League goalscorer with 17 goals?

75. Arsenal beat Spurs 3-1 at White Hart Lane in May 1999. Which three players scored the goals?

76. Which two goalkeepers were used during the 38 League games?

77. How many of the 38 Premier League games did Arsenal win?

78. Can you name the three League clubs that Arsenal beat during March 1999?

79. Arsenal beat Manchester United 3-0 at Highbury. Can you name the goalscorers?

80. Patrick Vieira scored three League goals, against which three clubs?

FRANK McLINTOCK

81. Where was Frank born - London, Manchester or Glasgow?

82. How many caps did Frank win for Scotland?

83. From which club did Arsenal sign Frank in 1964?

84. Which Arsenal manager brought Frank to Highbury?

85. In what year was Frank awarded 'Footballer of the Year'?

86. In April 1973 Frank left Arsenal and joined which club?

87. How many League goals did Frank score for Arsenal in his career?

88. In which year was Frank awarded the MBE?

89. At which club was Frank's first managerial appointment in 1977?

90. Which club did Frank manage between 1984 and 1987?

DAVID SEAMAN

91.   In what year was David born - 1961, 1962 or 1963?

92.   Which Midlands side did David play for during his career?

93.   How many England under-21 caps did David win for his country - 8, 10 or 12?

94.   From which club did Arsenal sign David in 1990?

95.   Which Arsenal manager signed David for the Gunners?

96.   Against which team did David make his League debut in August 1990?

97.   In David's first season at Arsenal he played in all 38 League games. Can you name three other players who also did this?

98.   During the 1993/1994 season David missed three Premier League games. Who played in goal for the Gunners in these games?

99.   Against which team did David make his 1000th career appearance in the FA Cup Semi-Final in April 2003?

100. In 2006, in which TV show did David participate, working closely with Jayne Torvill and Christopher Dean?

CHARITY/COMMUNITY SHIELD

101. *July 1999: Arsenal beat Man United 2-1 at Wembley. Who scored the goals?*

102. *August 1991: with which team did Arsenal share the trophy after drawing 0-0?*

103. *August 1979: which team beat Arsenal 3-1 to win the Charity Shield?*

104. *August 1998: which team did Arsenal beat 3-0, with Marc Overmars, Nicolas Anelka and Christopher Wreh scoring?*

105. *Which manager led Arsenal to win the Charity Shield in 1998?*

106. *August 1989: which team beat Arsenal 1-0 to win the Charity Shield?*

107. *August 2003: Arsenal played Manchester United in a 1-1 draw with Thierry Henry scoring. Where was the game played?*

108. *Who played in goal for Arsenal against Manchester United in the 2-1 win in 1999?*

109. *August 1993: Arsenal drew 1-1 with Manchester United. Who scored Arsenal's goal?*

110. *August 2002: Arsenal won the Community Shield 2-0, against who?*

LEAGUE CUP WINNERS - 1987

111. Which club did Arsenal beat in the Final?

112. What was the score in the game?

113. Who scored Arsenal's goal in the Final?

114. Which team did Arsenal beat in the Semi-Final?

115. Paul Davis scored two League goals against which clubs?

116. Which club did Arsenal knock out in the Quarter-Finals, winning 2-0 at Highbury?

117. Which London club did Arsenal beat 2-0 in the 4th round?

118. Which goalkeeper played in all nine League Cup matches?

119. Niall Quinn scored three League goals, against which clubs?

120. Which manager led Arsenal to this success?

PAT RICE

121. In what year was Pat born - 1947, 1948 or 1949?

122. What country did Pat request at full international level?

123. How many full caps did he win for his country - 45, 47 or 49?

124. When Pat left Arsenal, which club did he join?

125. How many appearances did Pat make for Arsenal - 510, 517 or 527?

126. Which team did Pat manage for two weeks as 'acting manager'?

127. Against which team did Pat score in the FA Cup 4th round in February 1972?

128. Against which team did Pat score on 30 December 1978 when Arsenal won 3-1?

129. Pat played in all 42 League matches in 1975/1976, scoring one goal. Who against?

130. How many League goals did Pat score for Arsenal?

THE FA CUP

131. Who scored Arsenal's goal in the 1993 Semi-Final 1-0 win against Tottenham Hotspur?

132. How many FA Cup trophies did Arsenal win under Terry Neill?

133. Who scored the only goal against Wolves in the FA Cup Semi-Final in April 1998 to reach the Final?

134. Which team did Arsenal beat 2-0 in the 1950 Final?

135. In 1980 how many Semi-Final replays did Arsenal play against Liverpool before reaching the Final?

136. Which London side did Arsenal beat 2-1 in the 2001 Semi-Final?

137. How many English players were in the starting eleven in the 2003 Final against Southampton?

138. In 2002 Arsenal beat Middlesbrough 1-0 in the Semi Final Where was the game played?

139. How many FA Cup trophies did Arsenal win under Bertie Mee?

140. Which team did Arsenal beat 2-0 in the 1930 Final?

BOB WILSON

141. In which year was Bob Wilson born - 1939, 1940 or 1941?

142. How many full Scotland caps did Bob win for his country?

143. In which year did Bob become an Arsenal player (as an amateur)?

144. Bob became injured during the 1972 FA Cup Semi-Final against Stoke City in the 1-1 draw. Who went in goal when Bob went off?

145. How many League appearances did Bob make for Arsenal - 134, 234 or 334?

146. Bob made his League debut at home to Nottingham Forest in August 1963. Which side was he playing for?

147. Whilst playing for Arsenal, which two medals did Bob win?

148. During the mid-1960s Bob was understudy to which goalkeeper?

149. In how many of Arsenal's nine FA Cup games during the 1971 success did Bob play?

150. What is the name of the charity that Bob and his wife started in 1999?

DENNIS BERGKAMP

151. In what year was Dennis born - 1967, 1968 or 1969?

152. From what club did Arsenal sign Dennis in 1995?

153. Against which club did Dennis score his first two Arsenal goals?

154. Dennis made his Arsenal League debut on 20 August 1995, against which club?

155. Which nationality is Dennis?

156. How many League goals did Dennis score in his first season at Highbury - 9, 10 or 11?

157. Dennis scored a hat-trick against which club in a 3-3 draw in August 1997?

158. Which manager brought Dennis to Highbury?

159. What does Dennis have a fear of that prevents him playing some European games?

160. On 11 May 2002 Dennis scored against Everton in a 4-3 win to see Arsenal presented with the title. Which other players scored for the Gunners?

ARSENAL
v. MANCHESTER UNITED

161. In March 1998, which Dutchman scored in a 1-0 Arsenal win at Old Trafford?

162. Arsenal beat United 2-0 in the FA Cup 5th round. Which players scored the goals?

163. What was the score when the sides met for the first time in the Premier League?

164. Which Alan scored twice in a 2-0 win over United in Division One in January 1979?

165. What was the score when the teams meet on the opening day of the League season in 1986?

166. Can you name the scorers when Arsenal beat United in the 1979 FA Cup Final?

167. Perry Groves scored in a 1-0 win in December at home, in what year?

168. In September 1998 Arsenal beat United 3-0 in the League. Who scored the goals?

169. In the 1990/1991 season United knocked out Arsenal, beating them 6-2, with Alan Smith scoring twice. Which competition?

170. On the opening day of the season in 1973 Arsenal beat Manchester United at Highbury 3-0. Which players scored the goals?

ALAN SUNDERLAND

171.　In what year was Alan born - 1949, 1951 or 1953?

172.　From what team did Arsenal sign Alan in November 1977?

173.　In 1979 Alan scored the winning goal against which team in the FA Cup Final?

174.　Which Arsenal manager brought Alan to Highbury?

175.　How many League appearances did Alan make for Arsenal?

176.　Against which London team did Alan score a hat-trick in a 5-0 win in December 1978?

177.　In what year did Alan win his only England cap?

178.　What team did Alan sign for when he left Highbury in 1984?

179.　Alan scored a hat-trick in the League Cup in September 1979 in a 7-0 win, against who?

180.　Against which East Anglian side did Alan score two goals in a 3-0 win in September 1983?

THIERRY HENRY

181. In what year was Thierry born – 1977, 1978 or 1979?

182. Which Italian side did Thierry sign from to join Arsenal?

183. In what year did Thierry join Arsenal?

184. In what season was Thierry voted 'Opta Player of the Season' and 'Golden Boot Winner'?

185. During 2000/2001 Thierry scored four Champion League goals. Can you name two of the four sides he scored against?

186. Against which club did Thierry score a hat-trick during 2000/2001?

187. Two League hat-tricks for Thierry within a week in April 2004. Name the two clubs.

188. Thierry scored two hat-tricks for the gunners during 2002/2003, one in the League and one in the Champions League. Can you name the two clubs?

189. During 2002/2003 Thierry scored a wonder goal, running 70 yards past players and slotted the ball home, against which club?

190. Whose record did Thierry break, making him Arsenal's highest ever goalscorer?

LEAGUE CUP WINNERS - 1993

191. Which club did Arsenal beat in the Final?

192. What was the score in the game?

193. Which two London clubs did Arsenal beat on their way to the Final?

194. Which players scored Arsenal's goals in the Final?

195. Which team did Arsenal beat 5-1 on aggregate in the Semi-Final?

196. Which defender scored Arsenal's goal in a 1-0 win at Scarborough in the 4th round?

197. Which player scored both goals in a 2-0 win in the 5th round against Nottingham Forest?

198. At what stadium was the Final played?

199. Can you name six of Arsenal's starting eleven that played in the Final?

200. Which manager led Arsenal to this success?

PAT JENNINGS

201. In what year was Pat born - 1941, 1943 or 1945?

202. What club did Pat sign from to join Arsenal?

203. How many full international caps did he win for Northern Ireland?

204. How many League appearances did Pat make for Arsenal?

205. Which manager sold Pat Jennings to Arsenal?

206. In what year was Pat awarded an OBE?

207. During the 1977/1978 season how many of Arsenal's 42 League matches did he play?

208. During the 1983/1984 season Pat missed four games. Who played in goal for the Gunners?

209. How many goals did Pat score for Arsenal?

210. What was the first medal Pat won at Highbury?

2002/2003

211. In what position in the Premier League did Arsenal finish?

212. Against which team did Arsenal play on the opening day of the season, winning 2-0?

213. Which side knocked Arsenal out of the League Cup, losing 3-2?

214. Arsenal beat Liverpool in the Community Shield. What was the score?

215. Against which two Dutch sides did Arsenal play in the Champions League run?

216. Against which London side did Thierry Henry score a hat-trick in a 3-1 win in January 2003?

217. Can you name the three goalkeepers that played for Arsenal during that season?

218. Which two players scored hat-tricks in the same game against Southampton in May 2003?

219. How many points did Arsenal have in the Premier League at the end of the season - 71, 73 or 78?

220. Which player scored a hat-trick against Sunderland on the final day of the season in a 4-0 win?

ROBERT PIRES

221. In what year was Robert born - 1971, 1972 or 1973

222. From which club did Arsenal sign Robert in 2000?

223. Against which club did Robert score a hat-trick during the 2002/2003 season?

224. Can you name the German side that Robert scored against in the Champions League during 2001/2002 in both matches?

225. What award did Robert win after the 2001/2002 season?

226. Robert scored the only goal to win Arsenal the 2003 FA Cup Final. Which club did Arsenal beat?

227. How many League goals did Robert score during 2001/2002 - 6, 7 or 9?

228. Arsenal beat Spurs 2-1 in the 2001 FA Cup Semi-Final, with Robert scoring. Which other Gunner scored?

229. During the 2003/2004 League season which London team did Robert score against both home and away?

230. Against which club did Robert make his Arsenal League debut in 2000?

ALAN BALL

231. In what year did Alan sign for Arsenal?

232. Alan was signed for a British record fee in 1971, from which club?

233. Can you name the team that Alan scored twice against, both at home and away, during 1974/1975?

234. How many League appearances did Alan make for Arsenal?

235. How many League goals did Alan score for Arsenal?

236. Which manager brought Alan to Highbury?

237. Alan made his Arsenal League debut against which club?

238. How many England caps did Alan win during his career?

239. When Alan left Arsenal which club did he join in December 1976?

240. At which club was Alan's first managerial appointment during the 1980/1981 season?

PAUL MARINER

241. In what year was Paul born - 1951, 1953 or 1955?

242. From which club did Arsenal sign Paul in February 1984?

243. Which Arsenal manager brought Paul to Highbury?

244. Paul played 15 games for Arsenal in his first season. How many goals did he score?

245. How many League goals did Paul score in his Arsenal career?

246. Arsenal beat Hereford in the FA Cup 3rd round replay 7-2. How many goals did Paul score?

247. How many England caps did Paul win in his career?

248. When Paul left Arsenal which club did he sign for on a free transfer?

249. On 2 March 1985 Arsenal beat West Ham 2-1. Paul scored one, but who scored the other?

250. Against which Midlands team did Paul score on the 10 November 1984 in a 1-1 draw?

MANAGER: ARSÈNE WENGER

251. In what year was Arsène born - 1947, 1948 or 1949?

252. In what year was Arsène appointed Arsenal manager?

253. Against which club was Arsène's first match in charge of Arsenal?

254. Which Japanese club had Arsène managed before his Arsenal managerial career?

255. Arsène was the first French manager to have done what?

256. What was Arsène's first trophy as Gunners manager?

257. In February 1997 which 18-year-old French striker did Arsène buy for Arsenal?

258. Which French club had Arsène managed before his Arsenal managerial career?

259. In the summer of 1997 which two players did Arsène sign from Monaco?

260. Who was Arsène's first signing for Arsenal?

EUROPEAN CUP WINNERS' CUP WINNERS - 1994

261. Which team did Arsenal beat in the Final?

262. What was the score in the game?

263. Which Arsenal player score in the Final?

264. Which French side did Arsenal beat 2-1 on aggregate in the Semi-Final?

265. Which club did Arsenal play in the 1st round of the competition?

266. Six Arsenal players scored against Standard Liege in a 7-0 away win. Can you name three of them?

267. Which team did Arsenal beat 1-0 on aggregate in the 3rd round, with Tony Adams scoring?

268. Who was the only used substitute for Arsenal in the Final?

269. Which goalkeeper played in all nine European games for the Gunners?

270. Which manager led Arsenal to this success?

PETER STOREY

271. In what year was Peter born - 1943, 1944 or 1945?

272. Against which team did Peter make his debut in October 1965?

273. Who was Arsenal's manager when Peter made his Arsenal debut?

274. During the 1970/1971 League Championship success Peter scored two goals, against who?

275. How many England caps did Peter win in his career?

276. Peter made 387 (4) League appearances for Arsenal, scoring how many goals - 7, 9 or 11?

277. Peter scored a derby goal in a 2-1 win over Tottenham in December 1972. Which other Gunner scored?

278. In March 1971 which team was 2-0 up over Arsenal in the FA Cup Semi-Final only for Peter to score two goals and force a replay?

279. Following on from the previous question, against which goalkeeper did he score those two goals?

280. Which London club did Peter join when he left Arsenal?

RAY KENNEDY

281. In what year did Ray make his Arsenal debut?

282. Against which team did Ray score League hat-tricks in a 4-0 home win in October 1970?

283. On 3 May 1971 Ray scored the goal against which team to hand the title to the Gunners?

284. Against which London team did Ray score two goals in a 3-1 away win in April 1974?

285. How many League goals did Ray score in his Arsenal career?

286. During the 1970/1971 season Ray played in 41 matches. How many goals did he score?

287. Against which two clubs did Ray score goals during this 1970/1971 FA Cup run?

288. Can you name three European sides that Ray scored against in the European Cup in 1971/1972?

289. Which team did Ray join when he left Arsenal in 1974?

290. How many England caps did Ray win in his career?

MALCOLM MACDONALD

291. In what year was Malcolm born - 1948, 1950 or 1952?

292. Malcolm joined Arsenal in August 1976, from which club?

293. How many League goals did Malcolm score in his 84 appearances?

294. Malcolm made nine FA Cup appearances for Arsenal. How many goals did he score?

295. Against which team did Malcolm make his Arsenal debut in a 1-0 home defeat?

296. Against which team did Malcolm score his first goal on 25 August 1976 in a 3-1 win?

297. Against which Midlands club did Malcolm score a hat-trick in a 3-3 draw in January 1977?

298. Against which county did Malcolm score five goals whilst playing for England in 1975?

299. How may England caps did Malcolm win in his career?

300. Which London club did Malcolm manage between 1980 and 1984?

JOHN RADFORD

301.   In what year was John born - 1945, 1946 or 1947?

302.   In December 1971, against which club did John score two goals in a 2-0 win?

303.   John scored in his first derby against Spurs, in what year?

304.   John was Player of the Year in 1968. In what other year did he win the award?

305.   How many derby goals did John score for Arsenal against Spurs in his career?

306.   Against which team did John have his debut?

307.   How many League goals did John score in his Arsenal career?

308.   What club did John join when he left Highbury?

309.   How many England caps did John win?

310.   Following on from the previous question, which countries were they against?

LEAGUE CHAMPIONS - 1990/1991

311. How many of the 38 League games did Arsenal win?

312. Four players played in every League game. Can you name them?

313. Which player was the leading goalscorer with 22 League goals?

314. Which two 'Pauls' both scored 13 League goals each?

315. David O'Leary scored one goal during the season, against who?

316. Which player scored a hat-trick against Manchester United in a 3-1 win in May 1991?

317. How many points did Arsenal finish with, having had two points deducted?

318. Anders Limpar scored a hat-trick against which club in a 6-1 win?

319. How many League games did Arsenal lose during the season?

320. Which manager guided Arsenal to this success?

PERRY GROVES

321. In what year was Perry born in London - 1963, 1964 or 1965?

322. Against which League teams did Perry score his three League goals during the 1986/1987 season?

323. On the opening day of the 1990/1991 season Perry came off the bench to score against which side in the 3-0 away win?

324. Perry passed a few defenders before laying on the winner for which player in the 1987 League Cup Final?

325. How many League goals did Perry score for Arsenal in his career?

326. Against which team did Perry score in February 1988 in the 1-0 League Cup Semi-Final, first League tie?

327. From which team did Perry sign to join Arsenal in 1986?

328. Perry is the nephew of which former Arsenal captain?

329. Which manager signed Perry for Arsenal?

330. When Perry left Arsenal in August 1992 who did he join?

TONY ADAMS

331. In what year was Tony born - 1962, 1964 or 1966?

332. How many England under-21 caps did Tony win - 3, 5 or 7?

333. In which year did Tony win 'Young Player of the Year'?

334. Tony took over from whom as captain during 1987/1988?

335. Tony made his League debut for Arsenal in November 1983, against who?

336. On 4 January 1987 Tony scored against which London side to help Arsenal win 2-1?

337. When Arsenal won the 'Double' in 1997/1998 Tony made 26 League appearances. How many goals did he score - 1, 2 or 3?

338. Tony made his England debut against Spain, in which year?

339. To which two trophies did Tony skipper Arsenal in 1993?

340. Which manager gave Tony his international debut for England?

MANAGER: DON HOWE

341. From whom did Don take over as Arsenal manager?

342. In what year was Don appointed Arsenal manager?

343. Which Arsenal manager brought Don to Highbury as a player?

344. Don made his Arsenal debut on the opening day of the 1964/1965 season, against which club?

345. In what year was Don born in Wolverhampton - 1934, 1935 or 1936?

346. In March 1966 Don broke his leg in a collision with which Blackpool goalkeeper?

347. How many League goals did Don score in his Arsenal playing career?

348. How many caps did he win for England - 21, 23 or 25?

349. Which London club did Don manage between 1989 and 1991?

350. In what position did Don play during his playing career?

PLAYERS NATONALITIES

Match the player with his nationality

351.	Anders Limpar	French
352.	Nwankwo Kanu	Dutch
353.	Steve Morrow	French
354.	Tony Adams	Croatian
355.	Davor Suker	English
356.	Marc Overmars	Northern Irish
357.	Robert Pires	Swedish
358.	Emmanuel Petit	Nigerian
359.	John Jensen	French
360.	Thierry Henry	Danish

ANDERS LIMPAR

361. Against which side did Anders score in the European Cup in September 1991 in a 6-1 home win?

362. What nationality is Anders?

363. Which manager brought Anders to Highbury in 1990?

364. From which Italian team did Arsenal sign Anders?

365. Anders made 96 League appearances for Arsenal. How many goals did he score?

366. Anders scored two League goals for Arsenal in their first Premier League season. Which sides were they against?

367. When Anders left Arsenal for £1.6 million who did he join?

368. Against which club did Anders score a 45-yard lob in April 1992?

369. During the 1990/1991 season Anders made 34 League appearances. How many goals did he score?

370. How many caps did Anders win for his country?

NIALL QUINN

371. Where was Niall born - Belfast, London or Dublin?

372. Against which club did Niall make his Arsenal debut in December 1985?

373. During the 1986/1987 season how many goals did Niall score in his 35 League appearances?

374. Against which two teams did Niall score his two League goals during 1987/1988?

375. Niall made 67 League appearances for Arsenal. How many goals did he score?

376. Which country did Niall represent at international level?

377. Against which three teams did Niall score to help Arsenal reach the 1987 League Cup Final?

378. Niall left Highbury in March 1990. Which club did he join?

379. Against which team did Niall score in April 1989 in a 2-0 League win?

380. During the 1989/1990 season Niall made six League appearances for the Gunners, scoring two goals, against who?

ASHLEY COLE

381. In what year was Ashley born - 1979, 1980 or 1981?

382. For which London team did Ashley play during 1999/2000 while on loan?

383. Ashley made his Arsenal debut in November 1999 in a League Cup tie, against which club?

384. Which Arsenal manager gave Ashley his Arsenal debut?

385. In 2005, which 'Girls Aloud' member did Ashley get engaged to?

386. Ashley made his England debut in March 2001, in a 3-1 away win against which country?

387. In the 2003/2004 season against which team did Ashley score in the Champions League?

388. Ashley made his Arsenal League debut in May 2000, against which club?

389. Which England manager gave Ashley his international debut?

390. How many Premiership goals did Ashley score during 2000/2001 - 3, 5 or 7?

ARSENAL v. CHELSEA

391. On Boxing Day 2002 Arsenal beat Chelsea 2-1 at
      Highbury. Who scored the goals?

392. During the 2003/2004 season Arsenal beat Chelsea 2-1
      both home and away. Which Arsenal player scored in
      both games?

393. Who scored the goals in the 2-0 FA Cup Final win in
      2002?

394. Which player scored a hat-trick for the Gunners at
      Stamford Bridge to win 3-2 in October 1999?

395. Who scored the only goal in a 1-0 win in January 1999?

396. Ian Wright and Paul Merson scored in a 2-1 Highbury
      win on 28 September, in what year?

397. In 2003/2004, other than in the League, what
      competition did the teams play?

398. In February 2001 which Gunner came from the bench to
      score two goals against Chelsea in the 3-1 FA Cup 5th
      round?

399. On 16 April 1979 Arsenal beat Chelsea 5-2. Who scored
      the goals?

400. On the opening day of the 1971/1972 season Arsenal
      beat Chelsea 3-0. Who scored the goals?

LEAGUE POSITIONS - 2

Match the season with the position that Arsenal finished

401.	2000/2001	Premiership	1st
402.	1995/1996	Premiership	17th
403.	1989/1990	Division One	7th
404.	1980/1981	Division One	2nd
405.	1975/1976	Division One	3rd
406.	1970/1971	Division One	5th
407.	1966/1967	Division One	11th
408.	1960/1961	Division One	1st
409.	1952/1953	Division One	1st
410.	1930/1931	Division One	4th

DAVID ROCASTLE

411. Where was David born - Manchester, London or Nottingham?

412. David scored in February 1988 in the League Cup Semi Final 2nd leg in the 3-1 win over Everton. Which other players scored?

413. What was David's nickname?

414. Against which two League clubs did David score during the 1986/1987 season?

415. How many League goals did David score for the Gunners?

416. How many England caps did David win for England?

417. Which Arsenal manager gave David his debut for Arsenal?

418. For which other London club did David play in his career?

419. In 1992 David left Arsenal. Which club did he join?

420. What award did David win as an Arsenal player in 1986?

PAUL MERSON

421. In what year was Paul born - 1966, 1968 or 1970?

422. Can you name the three clubs that Paul scored against in his first season at Highbury?

423. Which club did Paul join when he left Arsenal in 1997?

424. How many League goals did Paul score in his Arsenal career?

425. In April 1992 Paul scored a League hat-trick against which side, winning 4-1?

426. Paul played in all 42 League games during the 1991/1992 season. How many goals did he score - 10, 12 or 14?

427. What was Paul's nickname at Highbury?

428. For which team did Paul play during 1986/1987 whilst on loan?

429. In what year did Paul win PFA Young Player of the Year?

430. Paul made his Arsenal debut in November 1986, against which club?

SOL CAMPBELL

431. In what year was Sol born - 1972, 1974 or 1976?

432. Sol made his Arsenal debut in a 4-0 League win, against which club?

433. From which team did Sol sign to join Arsenal?

434. Which Arsenal manager signed Sol for the Gunners?

435. Against which country did Sol score his first England goal?

436. In what year did Sol join Arsenal?

437. Against which Midlands side did Sol score in the League in August 2003 in a 2-0 home win?

438. What was strange about Sol's England debut in February 1995 against the Republic of Ireland?

439. Sol scored two League goals in his first season at Highbury, against which clubs?

440. What trophies did Sol win in his first season at Highbury?

CHAMPIONS LEAGUE
FINALISTS - 2006

441. Against which team did Arsenal play in the Final?

442. What was the score in the game?

443. Who captained Arsenal for this match?

444. Who scored Arsenal's goal in the Final?

445. In what stadium was the final played?

446. Can you name seven of the starting eleven players for the Gunners?

447. Can you name Arsenal's three used substitutes in the Final?

448. Who played in goal for the Gunners and was the first ever player to be sent off in a Champions League Final?

449. Which players scored the goals against Arsenal in the Final?

450. Can you name the Norwegian referee who took charge of the Final?

NICOLAS ANELKA

451.   In what year was Nicolas born - 1977, 1978 or 1979?

452.   Which French side sold Nicolas to Arsenal for £500,000?

453.   Against which team did Nicolas score a League brace in April 1998?

454.   What nationality in Nicolas?

455.   In February 1999 Nicolas scored a League hat-trick against which club?

456.   When Nicolas left Highbury which club did he sign for?

457.   Nicolas scored Arsenal's second goal in the 1998 FA Cup Final, against which goalkeeper?

458.   Nicolas made his debut in April 1997 in a 3-0 win, against which club?

459.   From which French side did Manchester City sign Nicolas for £13 million in 2002?

460.   For which Premier League team did Nicolas play during the 2001/2002 season?

STEVE BOULD

461. In what year was Steve born - 1960, 1961 or 1962?

462. Steve made his Arsenal debut in 1988 in a 5-1 win, against who?

463. For which team did Steve play during 1982/1983 whilst on loan?

464. How many England caps did Steve win?

465. From which club did Steve sign to join Arsenal in 1988?

466. In which Cup Final was Steve 'Man of the Match' for Arsenal?

467. Steve scored two League goals during 1988/1989, against which clubs?

468. When Arsenal were crowned League Champions in 1998, in how many games did Steve play - 20, 22 or 24?

469. How many League Championship winners' medals did Steve win whilst at Highbury?

470. When Steve left Arsenal which club did he join?

WHERE DID THEY COME FROM?

Match the player with the club he signed from to join Arsenal

471.	Tommy Docherty	Norwich City
472.	Chris Kiwomya	Sporting Lisbon
473.	Brian Marwood	Dundee
474.	Bobby Gould	Manchester United
475.	Steve Williams	Sheffield Wednesday
476.	Jeff Blockley	Ipswich Town
477.	Andy Linighan	Preston North End
478.	Brian Kidd	Coventry City
479.	Luis Boa Morte	Southampton
480.	Ian Ure	Coventry City

PATRICK VIEIRA

481. In what year was Patrick born - 1972, 1974 or 1976?

482. From which club did Arsenal sign Patrick?

483. In what year did Patrick sign for Arsenal?

484. In what country was Patrick born?

485. Patrick made his Arsenal debut in 1996 at home, against which club?

486. For which international team did Patrick win caps?

487. For whom did Patrick provide the pass in the 1998 World Cup Final for the player to score against Brazil in a 3-0 win?

488. Which Arsenal manager signed Patrick for the Gunners?

489. How many Premiership title winners' medals did he win while at Arsenal?

490. Patrick left Arsenal in 2005. Which Italian side did he join?

LIAM BRADY

491. In what year was Liam born - 1956, 1957 or 1958?

492. Arsenal beat Manchester United in December 1976 with Liam scoring. Who scored the other two goals?

493. What was Liam's nickname at Highbury?

494. Liam scored two goals on the opening day of the season in August 1978 in a 2-2 draw, against who?

495. How many League goals did Liam score in his Arsenal career?

496. Can you name the four Italian clubs that Liam played for in his career?

497. How many caps did Liam win for the Republic of Ireland?

498. Which Scottish team did Liam manage between 1991 and 1993?

499. With which London club did Liam finish his playing career?

500. Liam played 37 League games during the 1978/1979 season. How many goals did he score?

FA CUP WINNERS - 1993

501. Which club did Arsenal beat in the Final (replay)?

502. What was the score in the Final (replay)?

503. Which players scored the goals in the Final (replay)?

504. Which team did Arsenal beat 1-0 in the Semi-Final at Wembley?

505. Arsenal drew 1-1 in the Final before the replay match. Who scored the Arsenal goal?

506. Which East Anglian side did Arsenal beat 4-2 in the Quarter-Final?

507. Ian Wright scored a hat-trick in the 3rd round in a 3-1 away win, against who?

508. Which Yorkshire side did Arsenal beat in the 4th round?

509. How many goals did Tony Adams score during the FA Cup run?

510. Which manager led Arsenal to this success?

RAY PARLOUR

511. In what year was Ray born - 1969, 1971 or 1973?

512. Against which club did Ray make his Arsenal debut in January 1992?

513. What was Ray's nickname while at Highbury?

514. When Arsenal did the 'Double' in 1998 Ray played in 34 League matches, scoring how many goals - 5, 6 or 7?

515. Ray was 'Man of the Match' in the 1998 FA Cup Final. Which side did Arsenal beat 2-0?

516. Against which club did Ray score against in a Cup Final in 2002?

517. How many League title winners' medals did Ray win whilst an Arsenal player?

518. Against which two sides did Ray score in the 2000/2001 Champions League?

519. How many England caps did Ray win for his country?

520. When Ray left Arsenal which club did he join?

LEAGUE GOALSCORERS
FOR ARSENAL - 1

Match the player with the number of League goals scored

521.	Jon Sammels	10
522.	David O'Leary	62
523.	Chris Kiwomya	17
524.	Kevin Richardson	39
525.	Derek Tapscott	3
526.	Alan Smith	11
527.	Gerry Ward	86
528.	Anders Limpar	59
529.	Tony Woodcock	5
530.	George Graham	56

TONY WOODCOCK

531.   Where was Tony born - London, Glasgow or Nottingham?

532.   From which club did Arsenal sign Tony?

533.   Which team did Tony sign for as an apprentice in 1974?

534.   Against which club did Tony score five goals in a 6-2 away win in October 1983?

535.   How many League goals did Tony score in his Arsenal career?

536.   Against which country did Tony make his international debut in 1978?

537.   Tony played in 34 League games during 1982/1983. How many goals did he score - 12, 13 or 14?

538.   How many England caps did Tony win during his career?

539.   When Tony left Highbury which German side did he join?

540.   How many England goals did Tony score for his country?

2003/2004

541. How many of the 38 League games did Arsenal win?

542. Thierry Henry scored two hat-tricks, against which clubs?

543. Who was the only player to start in all 38 League games?

544. Which Midlands club did Arsenal beat 2-0, both home and away?

545. Arsenal's biggest League win was 5-0 in April 2004, against who?

546. Arsenal won all four games in August 2003. Can you name two of the four opponents?

547. Thierry Henry was Arsenal's highest League scorer. How many goals did he score?

548. Arsenal beat Chelsea 2-1, both home and away. Which Arsenal player scored in both games?

549. Who did Arsenal play on the final day of the season to be crowned champions?

550. How many League games did Arsenal lose?

CHARLIE NICHOLAS

551. In what year was Charlie born in Glasgow - 1961, 1962 or 1963?

552. Against which team did Charlie score an FA Cup 3rd round hat-trick in January 1986?

553. Which Arsenal manager signed Charlie in 1983?

554. From which Scottish side did Arsenal sign Charlie?

555. Against which club did Charlie scored a brace in the League Cup Final in 1987?

556. How many Scottish caps did Charlie win?

557. Charlie made 151 League appearances for Arsenal. How many goals did he score - 30, 32 or 34?

558. Against which team did Charlie score his first two goal in his second League appearance for Arsenal in August 1983?

559. On Boxing Day 1983 Arsenal beat which team 4-2, with Charlie and Raphael Meade scoring two goals apiece?

560. When Charlie left Highbury in January 1988 which Scottish team did he sign for?

LEAGUE APPEARANCES
FOR ARSENAL

Match the player with the number of League appearances

561.	Brian Marwood	6 (2)
562.	Brian Talbot	1 (11)
563.	Neil Heaney	9 (7)
564.	John Hartson	52
565.	Mark Flatts	12 (3)
566.	Kevin Campbell	52 (8)
567.	Alan Miller	245 (9)
568.	Pal Lydersen	4 (3)
569.	Paul Mariner	124 (42)
570.	Paul Shaw	43 (10)

PETER SIMPSON

571. What was Peter's nickname at Highbury?

572. Peter made his Arsenal debut in March 1964, against who?

573. How many League goals did Peter score for Arsenal in his career?

574. Which three medals did Peter win while an Arsenal player?

575. In what year was Peter born - 1943, 1944 or 1945?

576. Against which League club did Peter score during 1973/1974, both home and away?

577. In what year did Peter win 'Player of the Year'?

578. Can you name the three Arsenal managers who Peter played under during his Gunners career?

579. Against which team did Peter score his only goal of the 1972/1973 season in a 5-2 home win in August 1972?

580. Peter scored against Manchester United in a 3-0 home win in April 1972. Which other players scored?

ARSENAL
v. TOTTENHAM HOTSPUR

581. Arsenal beat Spurs in both Semi-Final legs of the League Cup in 1987, by what scoreline?

582. Which Arsenal player made his Arsenal debut against Spurs on 8 February 1987?

583. In September 1988 Arsenal beat Spurs 3-2 at White Hart Lane in Division One. Which player scored the goals?

584. Which 'David' has played 35 derby games for the Gunners?

585. Who managed Arsenal between 1926 and 1938 and Tottenham Hotspur between 1946 and 1949?

586. In what year was Graham Rix's testimonial game against Spurs?

587. In their first Premier League meeting in December 1992, what was the score?

588. Paul Davis made his Arsenal debut against Spurs in what year?

589. In April 1985 Arsenal beat Spurs at White Hart Lane. What was the score in Division One?

590. Arsenal beat Spurs 4-0 in Division One in September 1967. Against which Spurs goalkeeper did the Gunners score?

CHARLIE GEORGE

591. In what year was Charlie born - 1949, 1950 or 1951?

592. When Charlie left Arsenal which club did he join?

593. How many League goals did Charlie score for Arsenal in his 133 appearances?

594. In February 1971 Charlie scored a 5th round FA Cup goal against Manchester City - a free kick after the City keeper handled outside the area. Who was the goa keeper?

595. Charlie scored the winning, extra-time goal in the 1971 FA Cup Final. Can you name the opposing goalkeeper and his team?

596. Can you name the three sides that Charlie scored against before reaching the FA Cup Final in May 1971?

597. In February 1972, against which team did Charlie score two goals in a 2-0 home win?

598. How many England caps did Charlie win in his career?

599. Who was the only Arsenal manager that Charlie played under?

600. Which London side did Arsenal beat on 3 May 1971 in a 1-0 away win, for the Gunners to be crowned champions?

VIV ANDERSON

601. In what year was Viv born - 1955, 1956 or 1957?

602. Against which team did Viv score in the League Cup Semi Final second leg in March 1987?

603. Viv was the first black player to have done what?

604. Viv made 120 League appearances for Arsenal. How many goals did he score?

605. Can you name the country against which Viv made his England debut in November 1978?

606. How many England caps did Viv win?

607. Against which two League teams did Viv score during the 1985/1986 season?

608. Viv scored two England goals. Can you name the two countries he scored against?

609. Viv made his Arsenal debut in August 1984, against which London side?

610. Which team did Viv manage in the 1993/1994 season?

LEAGUE APPEARANCES FOR ARSENAL

Match the player with the number of League appearances for the Gunners

611.	Liam Brady	*314*
612.	Andy Cole	*234*
613.	Frank McLintock	*0 (1)*
614.	Pat Jennings	*227 (8)*
615.	Paul Davis	*223 (2)*
616.	Bob Wilson	*312 (2)*
617.	Paul Merson	*523 (35)*
618.	David O'Leary	*237*
619.	Frank Stapleton	*331 (20)*
620.	Kenny Sansom	*289 (38)*

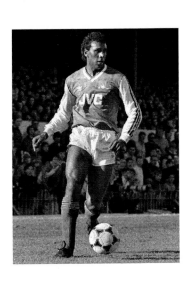

DAVID PLATT

621. In what year was David born - 1964, 1966 or 1968?

622. Arsenal paid which club £4.5 million for David?

623. David made his League debut on 20 August 1995 against Middlesbrough. What was the score?

624. David scored on his second League appearance for Arsenal on 23 August 1995, against which club?

625. How many England caps did David win for England?

626. How many goals did he score for England?

627. For which Midlands team did David play during his career?

628. David scored against Manchester United in a 3-2 home win in November 1997. Which other Arsenal players scored?

629. Can you name the three Italian clubs that David played for in his career?

630. When Arsenal did the 'Double' in 1998 David scored three League goals. Against which three clubs did he score?

LEAGUE CHAMPIONS - 1970/1971

631.   How many of their 42 League game did Arsenal win?

632.   Who scored a hat-trick in a 4-0 win against Nottingham Forest in October 1970?

633.   With how many points did Arsenal win the Championship - 61, 63 or 65?

634.   How many players were used during the season?

635.   Which manager guided Arsenal to this success?

636.   Which three players started all 42 League games?

637.   Arsenal recorded three 4-0 victories. Which clubs were they against?

638.   Who was the top scorer with 19 League goals?

639.   Which East Anglian side did Arsenal beat both home and away?

640.   Which London club did Arsenal beat 1-0, with Charlie George scoring the goal on the last day of the season?

PAUL DAVIS

641. Where was Paul born - Manchester, Glasgow or London?

642. In December 1984 against which Midlands team did Paul score in a 4-0 win?

643. During Arsenal's championship success of 1988/1989 Paul scored one League goal, against who?

644. For which club did Paul make five appearances during the 1995/1996 season?

645. In December 1994 Paul scored a goal in his last appearance for Arsenal in a 2-2 draw, against who?

646. In what year did Paul leave Arsenal?

647. During the 1992/1993 season Paul was involved in only six League matches, but played in two Cup Finals - in what competitions?

648. Paul's first derby appearance was in April 1980. What number shirt did he wear?

649. Charlie Nicolas, Martin Hayes (2) and Paul scored in a 4-1 home win against which club in April 1987?

650. What Arsenal manager gave Paul his debut for the Gunners?

LEE DIXON

651. Where was Lee born - London, Edinburgh or Manchester?

652. From which club did Arsenal sign Lee?

653. How many England caps did Lee win for England?

654. Which manager brought Lee to Arsenal?

655. Lee made his Arsenal debut in February 1988 in a 2-1 home win against which club?

656. For which team did Lee play during the 1985/1986 season?

657. Lee scored three League penalties during the 1989/1990 season, against which clubs?

658. Lee made his international debut for England at Wembley Stadium in 1990 against which country?

659. Which England manager gave Lee his first international cap?

660. How many League titles winners' medals did Lee win while at Arsenal?

THE CHAMPIONS LEAGUE

661. Against which English side did Arsenal play during 2003/2004?

662. Thierry Henry played 12 games for Arsenal in 2002/2003. How many goals did he score?

663. During the 1999/2000 season where did Arsenal play their home games?

664. Against which Spanish club did Arsenal play during the 1999/2000 Champions League?

665. In September 2002 which Dutch team did Arsenal beat 4-0?

666. Which goalkeeper played in every game in the 2003/2004 season?

667. Which team knocked Arsenal out of the 2000/2001 competition on away goals in the Quarter-Finals?

668. On 25 November 2003 Arsenal beat Inter Milan 5-1. Who scored the goals?

669. Can you name the four goalkeepers that played in the 2000/2001 Champions League for Arsenal?

670. During 2002/2003 against which Italian side did Thierry Henry score a hat-trick in a 3-1 away win?

EMMANUEL PETIT

671.   In which year was Emmanuel born - 1970, 1971 or
        1972?

672.   Emmanuel signed for Arsenal in the summer of 1997,
        from which club?

673.   Against which team did Emmanuel score his first Arsenal
        goal?

674.   What nationality is Emmanuel?

675.   Against which team did Emmanuel make his debut in
        August 1997?

676.   In what year did Emmanuel score in a World Cup Final,
        beating Brazil?

677.   On 5 May 1999 Emmanuel scored a derby goal against
        Spurs. Which two players scored the other goals for the
        Gunners?

678.   On the opening day of the 1998/1999 season Arsenal
        beat Nottingham Forest 2-1. Emmanuel scored on of the
        goals, but which Gunner scored the other?

679.   Against which team did Emmanuel score two goals in the
        FA Cup in January 1999?

680.   When Emmanuel left Arsenal which team did he join?

LEAGUE POSITIONS - 3

Match the season with the position that Arsenal finished

681.	2002/2003	Premiership	7th
682.	1997/1998	Premiership	4th
683.	1993/1994	Premiership	5th
684.	1983/1984	Division One	1st
685.	1976/1977	Division One	2nd
686.	1968/1969	Division One	10th
687.	1955/1956	Division One	3rd
688.	1919/1920	Division One	4th
689.	1913/1914	Division Two	6th
690.	1900/1901	Division Two	8th

WILLIE YOUNG

691. Where was Willie born - London, Glasgow or Edinburgh?

692. From which club did Arsenal sign Willie in 1977?

693. Which manager signed Willie for his previous club and for Arsenal?

694. How many League goals did Willie score for Arsenal?

695. In what position did Willie play for Arsenal?

696. For which East Anglian side did Willie play during 1983/1984?

697. In March 1978 Willie scored in a 4-0 home win against West Bromwich Albion. Which Arsenal player scored a hat-trick in the game?

698. Against which Welsh team did Willie score in a 3-2 FA Cup Quarter-Final tie in March 1978?

699. When Willie left Highbury after a disagreement with Terry Neill which club did he join?

700. Can you name the three League teams that Willie scored against in the 1979/1980 season?

ARSENAL HISTORY - 1

701. In 2001/2002 22 Arsenal players won a championship medal. How many goalkeepers did this include?

702. Who is Arsenal's most capped player, with 79 caps for France whilst an Arsenal player?

703. Can you name the two years in which Arsenal have clinched the League title at White Hart Lane?

704. Francesc Fabregas is Arsenal's youngest ever player, making his debut at 16 years and 177 days against which club in the League Cup in October 2003?

705. Which Arsenal captain has lifted more trophies than any other in the club's history?

706. Arsenal's first ever game at Highbury was in Sepetember 1913, against which team?

707. Which player (opponent) was the first ever to score at the Emirates Stadium in a League match in 2006?

708. Arsenal's record home attendance is 73,707 against RC Lens in November 1998, but the game was not played at Highbury. Where was it played?

709. The biggest attendance for an Arsenal game at Highbury is 73,295. Who did Arsenal play in this match in March 1935?

710. Arsenal set an English record between May 2001 and November 2002 by scoring in how many consecutive games?

JOHN JENSEN

711.   In what year was John born - 1961, 1963 or 1965?

712.   What nationality is John?

713.   Against which team did John score his first Arsenal goal?

714.   How many goals did John score for Arsenal in his career?

715.   Against which club did John make his debut in August 1992?

716.   In how many of Arsenal's 42 League games during 1992/1993 did he play?

717.   How many League appearances did John make for Arsenal in his career?

718.   Which Arsenal manager signed John for the Gunners?

719.   In 1993, when Arsenal won both the FA Cup and League Cup, for which Final did John make the starting eleven?

720.   When John left Highbury in March 1996 which club did he sign for?

MARC OVERMARS

721. In what year was Marc born - 1971, 1972 or 1973?

722. From which Dutch side did Marc sign to join the Gunners?

723. On 20 November 1999 Marc scored a League hat-trick in a 5-1 win, against which club?

724. Which Arsenal manager signed Marc for the Gunners?

725. Against which team did Marc score in the 1998 FA Cup Final?

726. When Arsenal got the 'Double' in 1998 Marc made 32 League appearances. How many goals did he score?

727. Can you name the three Dutch sides that Marc played for before joining Arsenal?

728. On 9 August 1998 Marc scored in the Charity Shield match against Manchester United. What was the score?

729. Marc made his Arsenal League debut in August 1997, against which club?

730. During the 1998/1999 season against which League team did Marc score, both home and away?

2005/2006

731.   On the opening day of the League season Arsenal beat which club 2-0, with Thierry Henry and Robin Van Persie scoring?

732.   Which player played in all 38 League matches?

733.   When Arsenal beat Fulham in the League in August 2005 which two players scored two apiece in a 4-1 win?

734.   When Tottenham and Arsenal met in the League at White Hart Lane Ledley King scored to open the scoring. Which Gunner equalised to make the result 1-1?

735.   Thierry Henry appeared in 32 League games, scoring how many goals?

736.   In February 2006 Arsenal become the first English club to beat which Spanish team at their ground in the Champions League?

737.   In what position in the League did the Gunners finish?

738.   How many of the 38 League games did the Gunners win - 19, 20 or 21?

739.   In January 2006 Arsenal smashed seven goals in a 7-0 League win against Middlesbrough. Who were the scorers?

740.   Thierry Henry scored a hat-trick on the last day of the season against which club in a 4-2 win?

GRAHAM RIX

741. In what year was Graham born - 1953, 1955 or 1957?

742. How many England under-21 caps did Graham win - 3, 5 or 7?

743. How may full England caps did Graham win for his country?

744. Graham made 351 League appearances for Arsenal. How many goals did he score?

745. In what year did Graham sign for Arsenal as an apprentice?

746. Which team did Grahm manage between 2001 and 2002?

747. Graham was handed his England debut in 1981 by which manager?

748. For which London club did Graham play six games while on loan in 1987?

749. For which two French clubs did Graham play after he left Arsenal?

750. Which Scottish team did he take over as manager during the 2005/2006 season?

ARSENAL v. WEST HAM UNITED

751. What was the score when the sides met for the first time in the Premier League in November 1993?

752. Which Gunner scored a hat-trick in the 6-1 win in March 1976?

753. Which Arsenal striker scored both goals in a 2-0 away win in March 1992?

754. Who scored Arsenal's goals in their 4-0 home win in September 1997?

755. Arsenal beat West Ham United 2-1 at Upton Park in January 1998 in the League Cup Quarter-Final. Who scored the goals?

756. Which two players scored the goals in the 2-0 home win in the League in August 1996?

757. Who scored the only goal for West Ham United in the 1-0 defeat in the 1980 FA Cup Final?

758. In the 'Double' season 1970/1971 what was the score between the clubs at Highbury in January 1971?

759. Which Arsenal players scored in a 3-3 League draw with the Hammers on 7 May 1984?

760. Which Welsh striker scored the only goal for Arsenal in a 1-0 League win at Upton Park in February 1996?

LEAGUE GOALSCORERS
FOR ARSENAL - 2

Match the player with the number of League goals scored

761.	Liam Brady	11
762.	Charlie George	3
763.	David Rocastle	43
764.	Steve Walford	41
765.	Alan Sunderland	24
766.	Paul Dickov	51
767.	Graham Rix	5
768.	Willie Young	3
769.	Andy Linighan	31
770.	Peter Goring	55

FA CUP WINNERS - 1979

771. Which club did Arsenal beat in the Final?

772. What was the score in the Final?

773. Who scored Arsenal's goals in the Final?

774. How many 3rd round replays did Arsenal play against Sheffield Wednesday?

775. Arsenal beat Wolves 2-0 in the Semi-Final. Where was the game played?

776. Which team did Arsenal beat in the Quarter-Final reply 2-0?

777. Which goalkeeper played in all of Arsenal's eleven FA Cup games?

778. Arsenal beat Nottingham Forest 1-0 in the 5th round. Who scored the goal?

779. In which stadium was the FA Cup Final held?

780. Which manager led Arsenal to this success?

FRANK STAPLETON

781.   In what year was Frank born - 1954, 1955 or 1956?

782.   During the 1978/1979 FA Cup run Frank scored six goals. Can you name three of the five sides he scored against?

783.   Against which London side did Frank score the only goal in a 1-0 win during April 1979?

784.   For which Dutch side did Frank play during his playing career?

785.   How many League goals did Frank score in his playing career?

786.   When Frank left Arsenal in 1981 which club did he join?

787.   During August 1980 the Gunners beat Spurs 2-0 at Highbury. Frank scored one goal, but who scored the other?

788.   How many caps did Frank win for the Republic of Ireland?

789.   Frank scored a League hat-trick during 1978/1979, against which club?

790.   Which team did Frank manage between 1991 and 1994?

GEORGE ARMSTRONG

791.   In what year was George born - 1942, 1944 or 1946?

792.   In February 1962 George made his Arsenal League debut, against which club?

793.   Before becoming a professional footballer what apprenticeship did he complete?

794.   What was George's nickname whilst at Highbury?

795.   How many League goals did George score for Arsenal?

796.   In what year was George voted 'Player of the Year'?

797.   On 5 September 1970 George scored two goals in a 2-0 win, against who?

798.   How many League appearances did George make for Arsenal - 400, 500 or 600?

799.   In what year did George made his derby debut?

800.   George left Arsenal in 1977.Which club did he join?

FA CUP WINNERS - 1971

801. Which club did Arsenal beat in the Final?

802. What was the score in the Final?

803. Who scored Arsenal's goals in the Final?

804. Which club did Arsenal beat in the Semi-Finals?

805. Which goalkeeper played in every FA Cup game during this season for the Gunners?

806. How many goals did Charlie George score during the FA Cup?

807. Which club did Arsenal beat 3-0 in the 3rd round, with Radford scoring two and Ray Kennedy the other?

808. Can you name three of the five clubs that Arsenal beat to reach the Final?

809. Who played in goal for the opponents in the Final?

810. Which manager guided Arsenal to this success?

1992/1993 - FIRST PREMIER LEAGUE SEASON

811. In what position in the League did Arsenal finish?

812. Against which club was Arsenal's first League game on 15 August 1992?

813. Following on from the last question, what was the score in the game?

814. Arsenal beat two clubs 3-0 during the season. Name them.

815. Can you name the two goalkeepers that played for the Gunners during the season?

816. How many goals did Arsenal score during the League season?

817. Ian Wright was Arsenal's top leading scorer during the season. How many goals did he score?

818. Who scored six League goals during the season?

819. Who was Arsenal's manager during this season?

820. How many of the 42 League games did Arsenal win?

FREDDIE LJUNGBERG

821. In what year was Freddie born - 1975, 1976 or 1977?

822. Freddie made his League debut in a 3-0 win and scored, against which club?

823. What nationality is Freddie?

824. In what year did Freddie join Arsenal?

825. How many League goals did Freddie score during 2004/2005?

826. During 2005/2006 what squad number did Freddie wear?

827. Can you name Freddie's previous Swedish club?

828. During 2000/2001 Freddie featured in 30 League games, scoring how many goals - 4, 5 or 6?

829. Which Arsenal manager signed Freddie for the Gunners?

830. Freddie made his international debut in January 1998, against which country?

LEAGUE CHAMPIONS - 2001/2002

831. How many of their 38 League games did Arsenal win?

832. Thierry Henry made 33 League appearances. How many goals did he score?

833. Which Swedish midfielder scored 12 League goals?

834. Which club did Arsenal beat 4-0 on the opening day of the season?

835. Edu scored one League goal during the season, against who?

836. Arsenal's biggest League win of the season was in August 2001, against who?

837. Following on from the previous question, what was the score in the game?

838. Arsenal only lost three League games during the season. Which three teams defeated the Gunners?

839. Sol Campbell scored two goals during the season, against which clubs?

840. Against which club did Arsenal play on the final day of the season, winning 4-3?

KEVIN CAMPBELL

841. In what year was Kevin born - 1968, 1969 or 1970?

842. Kevin played 89 reserve matches for Arsenal, scoring how many goals - 94, 95 or 96?

843. During the 1988/1989 and 1989/1990 seasons Kevin spent time on loan at two clubs. Name them.

844. Which manager handed Kevin his Arsenal debut?

845. How many League goals did Kevin score for Arsenal?

846. In September 1993 Kevin scored a hat-trick in a 4-0 home win, against which club?

847. Kevin scored the winning goal in the European Cup Winners' Cup Semi-Final 2nd leg in April 1994, against which club?

848. In December 1993 Kevin scored a League hat-trick against Swindon Town. What was the score in the game?

849. During the 1992/1993 season Kevin made 37 League appearances, scoring four goals. Which clubs were they against?

850. When Kevin left Arsenal which team did he join?

LEAGUE GOALSCORERS
FOR ARSENAL - 3

Match the player with the number of League goals scored

851.	Ian Wright	98
852.	Joe Hulme	125
853.	Alan Smith	107
854.	Reg Lewis	124
855.	Jimmy Brain	128
856.	Joe Baker	150
857.	Ted Drake	75
858.	Jack Lambert	93
859.	Frank Stapleton	103
860.	Cliff Bastin	86

DAVID PRICE

861.   In what year was David born - 1953, 1954 or 1955?

862.   In December 1978 David scored the only goal in a 1-0
       win, against who?

863.   During the 1976/1977 season David scored one League
       goal for Arsenal, against who?

864.   Which manager signed David for Arsenal?

865.   How many League goals did David score for Arsenal?

866.   To which team did Arsenal loan David during
       1974/1975?

867.   David played in four Cup Finals for Arsenal. How many
       winners' medals did he end up with?

868.   Which team did David join when he left Highbury in
       March 1981?

869.   During the 1977/1978 season David scored a goal
       against Chelsea in a 3-0 win. Who scored the others?

870.   With which London team did David finish his playing
       career in the 1982/1983 season?

SAMMY NELSON

871. In what year was Sammy born - 1947, 1949 or 1951?

872. Against which club did Sammy make his League debut in October 1969?

873. Sammy scored three League goals during 1976/1977, against which clubs?

874. Sammy scored a fantastic goal in a 7-0 League win in 1979, against which club?

875. During November 1978 Sammy scored in a 4-1 home win against Ipswich. Which Gunner scored a hat-trick in the game?

876. How many League goals did Sammy score for Arsenal?

877. In what year did Sammy play in a winning FA Cup Final for Arsenal?

878. Sammy was a Northern Ireland international. How many caps did he win?

879. When Sammy left Arsenal in 1981 which club did he join?

880. Sammy scored one FA Cup goal in his Arsenal career, in January 1980 in a 2-0 win, against which club?

LEAGUE CHAMPIONS - 1997/1998

881. Arsenal played 38 League games. How many did they win?

882. Which team finished runners-up to the Gunners?

883. Who was Arsenal's top League scorer with 16 goals?

884. Arsenal recorded two 5-0 wins, against which clubs?

885. Which player scored a hat-trick against Leicester City in a 3-3 draw in August 1997?

886. Which Dutch player scored twelve League goals in 32 League appearances?

887. How many points did Arsenal win from their two games against Spurs?

888. Which two goalkeepers played in the 38 games (between them) during the season?

889. Which manager guided Arsenal to this success?

890. Arsenal lost their last two League games, against which clubs?

KENNY SANSOM

891. In what year was Kenny born - 1956, 1957 or 1958?

892. Terry Neill signed Kenny in August 1980, from which club?

893. Which two players did Arsenal part exchange for Kenny plus £1 million?

894. How many England caps did Kenny win?

895. Against which country did Kenny make his international debut in 1979?

896. What did Arsenal teammates nickname Kenny at Highbury?

897. In what year did Kenny win 'Player of the Year' at Highbury?

898. Kenny made 314 League appearances for Arsenal. How many goals did he score?

899. Kenny's first derby against Spurs was in 1980. What was the score?

900. On Kenny's birthday, 26 September 1987, he scored in a 1-0 win, having not scored for three years. Which club was that against?

NIGEL WINTERBURN

901. In what year was Nigel born - 1963, 1964 or 1965?

902. From what club did Arsenal sign Nigel?

903. Nigel made his England debut in 1989, against which country?

904. How many England caps did Nigel win for his country?

905. During the 1988/1989 season Nigel scored three League goals. Name the three teams he scored against?

906. What was Nigel's nickname at Highbury?

907. Against which club did Nigel make his Arsenal debut in Novemer 1987 in a 1-0 home defeat?

908. During 1991/1992 Nigel scored one League goal, against who?

909. Nigel scored against Oldham Athletic in 1992/1993. What was the score in the away game?

910. When Nigel left Highbury which London side did he join?

MANAGER: TERRY NEILL

911. In what year was Terry born in Belfast - 1938, 1940 or 1942?

912. At what young age was Terry made Arsenal captain?

913. What team did Terry manage before Arsenal?

914. In August 1977 Terry brought which goalkeeper from Spurs for the Gunners?

915. In November 1980 which Arsenal legend did Terry sell to Watford for £8,000?

916. How many Northern Ireland caps did Terry win - 51, 55 or 59?

917. Which manager did Terry take over from in 1976 at Highbury?

918. In 1981 Terry bought Peter Nicholas for £400,000 from which club?

919. When Terry left Arsenal as a player which club did he join?

920. In 1979 which player did Terry purchase for the Gunners from Ipswich Town for £450,000?

MARTIN KEOWN

921. In what year was Martin born - 1964, 1965 or 1966?

922. Against which country did Martin make his England debut in February 1992?

923. How many England caps did Martin win - 40, 43 or 46?

924. Martin re-signed for Arsenal in February 1993 for £2 million, from which club?

925. Why did Martin not play in the 1993 FA Cup and League Cup Finals for the Gunners?

926. In December 1994 Martin scored against which club in the League?

927. Which England manager gave Martin his England debut?

928. For which team did Martin play during 1985/1986 in Division One?

929. Martin left Highbury in July 2004 on a free transfer. Which club did he sign for?

930. During 1998/1999 Martin scored one League goal for the Gunners. Which team did he score against?

LEAGUE CHAMPIONS - 1988/1989

931. How many of the 38 League games did Arsenal win?

932. Three players started every League game. Name them.

933. Alan Smith scored a hat-trick on the opening day of the season, against who?

934. Alan Smith was the top League scorer, with how many goals?

935. How many players did Arsenal use during the season?

936. Arsenal's biggest win was 5-0, against who?

937. Arsenal beat Spurs 3-2 in September 1988. Who scored the goals?

938. Which club was the only team to beat Arsenal both home and away?

939. Who did Arsenal beat 2-0 on the final day of the season?

940. Following on from the last question, who scored the goals?

MANAGER: BRUCE RIOCH

941. In what year was Bruce appointed manager of Arsenal?

942. Which manager did Bruce replace at Highbury?

943. What club did Bruce leave to join Arsenal?

944. One of Bruce's first signings as boss of Arsenal was the
England captain. Name him.

945. Which player did Bruce bring to Arsenal from Inter
Milan, costing £7.5 million?

946. Who was Bruce's last signing as Arsenal manager?

947. In what position in the League did Arsenal finish in
Bruce's first season in charge?

948. At which club was Bruce's first managerial appointment?

949. Which international team did Bruce captain in the 1978
World Cup Finals?

950. In Bruce's first season at Highbury he led Arsenal to the
League Cup Semi-Final before getting knocked out by
which team on away goals?

ALAN SMITH

951.   In what year was Alan born - 1960, 1961 or 1962?

952.   How many caps did Alan win for England?

953.   From which club did Arsenal sign Alan in 1987?

954.   How many League championships did Alan win whilst at Highbury?

955.   Alan scored the only goal against which club to help Arsenal win the Cup Winners' Cup in 1994?

956.   During May 1991 Alan scored a hat-trick in a 3-1 win, against which side?

957.   In September 1991 Alan scored four goals in a 6-1 European Cup win at home, against which side?

958.   On 29 August 1987 Alan scored a hat-trick in a 6-0 home win, against which club?

959.   Alan scored three League goals during 1993/1994, against which three clubs?

960.   On the opening day of the 1988/1989 season Alan scored a hat-trick in a 5-1 away win, against which club?

ARSENAL - HISTORY - 2

961. Which manager guided Arsenal to their first ever trophy in 1930?

962. Which player played 172 consecutive games (a club record) between April 1926 and December 1929?

963. Who was the first ever Arsenal player to score a League goal at the Emirates Stadium in a 1-1 draw in 2006?

964. Who is the youngest player in the Gunners' history to be used in an FA Cup tie?

965. Who is the oldest player to be used in a Premier League game for Arsenal?

966. Gilberto scored the fastest ever Champions League goal against PSV Eindhoven. After how many seconds was this - 10, 20 or 30?

967. Arsenal's biggest League win was 12-0 in 1900. Who was this against?

968. During 2001/2002 Arsenal become the first Premier League team to have done what in a Premier League season?

969. Which Dutch player scored twice in a 2-1 away win against Charlton in September 2006, (one goal being a fantastic volley)?

970. What was Highbury's capacity in 2006 - 37,419, 38,419 or 39,419?

FA CUP WINNERS - 2002

971. Which club did Arsenal beat in the Final?

972. What was the score in the game?

973. Which players scored the goals in the Final?

974. Which goalkeeper played in goal for the FA Cup Final?

975. Can you name three of the five named subsitutes for the Final?

976. Arsenal beat Watford in the 3rd round. Who scored the four goals?

977. Which team did Arsenal beat 1-0 in the Semi-Final?

978. Dennis Bergkamp scored in a 1-0 win in the 4th round, against who?

979. Arsenal beat Newcastle United 3-0 in the Quarter-Final replay. Which players scored the goals?

980. Arsenal played Gillingham in the 5th round at Highbury. What was the score?

BOB McNAB

981. In what year was Bob born - 1942, 1943 or 1944?

982. From which club did Arsenal sign Bob in 1966?

983. Which club did Bob turn down, joining Arsenal instead?

984. How many League goals did Bob score in his Arsenal career?

985. Bob made his England debut in 1968, against which country?

986. How many England caps did Bob win - 2, 4 or 6?

987. In what position did Bob play for the Gunners?

988. In July 1975 Bob left Arsenal and joined which club?

989. How many goals did Bob score for Arsenal in his career (League and Cup)?

990. Against which East Anglian club did Bob score in a 4-0 away win in September 1973?

FA CUP WINNERS - 1998

991.   Which club did Arsenal beat in the Final?

992.   What was the score in the game?

993.   Which players scored the goals in the Final?

994.   At which stadium was the Final played?

995.   Which team did Arsenal beat in the Semi-Final at Villa Park?

996.   Against which two London clubs did Arsenal play in the FA Cup run?

997.   Who was the Arsenal captain during this success?

998.   Which two goalkeepers were used during Arsenal's success?

999.   What team did Arsenal play in the 3rd round?

1000. Which club did Arsenal beat 2-1 in the 4th round?

ANSWERS

DAVID O'LEARY

1.   1958
2.   Republic of Ireland
3.   Leeds United
4.   68
5.   Burnley
6.   558: 523 (35)
7.   11
8.   Crystal Palace (home), 4-0
9.   League Cup (Sheffield Wednesday)
10. Leeds United

THE LEAGUE CUP

11. Alan Sunderland
12. West Ham and Chelsea
13. Ian Wright
14. Manchester United
15. Michael Thomas
16. 2 in 1987 and 1993
17. Ian Wright and Dennis Bergkamp
18. 1987 (2-1 win v. Liverpool)
19. Charlie Nicholas
20. Pat Jennings

IAN WRIGHT

21. 1963
22. Crystal Palace
23. £2.5 million
24. 184
25. Sheffield Wednesday
26. 15
27. Paul Merson
28. Southampton (away), 4-0 win
29. 8
30. Aston Villa (away), 0-1

BRIAN TALBOT

31. 1953

32.	Ipswich Town
33.	Watford
34.	West Bromwich Albion
35.	Noddy
36.	Terry Neill
37.	40
38.	Gordon McQueen and Sammy McIlroy
39.	Liverpool
40.	7

ARSENAL: THE SUCCESS

41.	League Champions, Won 22, Pts 76	1989
42.	FA Cup Winners, 2-0 v. Chelsea	2002
43.	FA Cup Winners, 2-0 v. Huddersfield Town	1930
44.	League Champions, Won 23, Pts 91	1998
45.	League Champions, Won 28, Pts 66	1931
46.	FA Cup Winners, 1-0 v. Southampton	2003
47.	League Cup Winners, 2-1 v. Sheffield Wednesday	1993
48.	FA Cup Winners, 2-0 v. Liverpool	1950
49.	FA Cup Winners, 3-2 v. Manchester United	1979
50.	European Cup Winners' Cup Winners, 1-0 v. Palma	1994

MANAGER: GEORGE GRAHAM

51.	2
52.	The League Cup
53.	Bertie Mee
54.	Tommy Baldwin
55.	Millwall
56.	12
57.	1
58.	Crystal Palace
59.	Leeds United
60.	59

LEAGUE POSITIONS - 1

61.	2001/2002	Premier League	1st
62.	1999/2000	Premier League	2nd
63.	1996/1997	Premier League	3rd

64.	1992/1993	Premier League	10th
65.	1982/1983	Division One	10th
66.	1981/1982	Division One	5th
67.	1973/1974	Division One	10th
68.	1961/1962	Division One	10th
69.	1954/1955	Division One	9th
70.	1951/1952	Division One	3rd

1998/1999

71. Nottingham Forest
72. Middlesbrough
73. 2nd
74. Nicolas Anelka
75. Emmanuel Petit, Nicolas Anelka and Nwankwo Kanu
76. David Seaman and Alex Manninger
77. 22
78. Sheffield Wednesday, Everton and Coventry
79. Tony Adams, Nicolas Anelka and Freddie Ljungberg
80. Leeds United (home), Wimbledon (home) and Middlesbrough (away)

FRANK McLINTOCK

81. Glasgow
82. 9
83. Leicester City
84. Billy Wright
85. 1971
86. Queens Park Rangers
87. 26
88. 1972
89. Leicester City
90. Brentford

DAVID SEAMAN

91. 1963
92. Birmingham City
93. 10
94. Queens Park Rangers

95. George Graham
96. Wimbledon
97. Steve Bould, Lee Dixon and Nigel Winterburn
98. Alan Miller
99. Sheffield United
100. Dancing on Ice

CHARITY/COMMUNITY SHIELD
101. Ray Parlour and Nwankwo Kanu (pen.)
102. Tottenham Hotspur
103. Liverpool
104. Manchester United
105. Arsène Wenger
106. Liverpool
107. The Millennium Stadium, Cardiff
108. Alex Manninger
109. Ian Wright
110. Liverpool

LEAGUE CUP WINNERS - 1987
111. Liverpool
112. 2-1
113. Charlie Nicholas
114. Tottenham Hotspur
115. Huddersfield Town and Manchester City
116. Nottingham Forest
117. Charlton Athletic
118. John Lukic
119. Huddersfield Town, Charlton Athletic and Tottenham Hotspur
120. George Graham

PAT RICE
121. 1949
122. Northern Ireland
123. 49
124. Watford
125. 527: 520 (7)
126. Arsenal

127. *Reading, in a 2-1 win*
128. *Birmingham City*
129. *Sheffield United*
130. *12*

THE FA CUP

131. *Tony Adams*
132. *1, in 1979*
133. *Christopher Wreh*
134. *Liverpool*
135. *3*
136. *Tottenham Hotspur*
137. *4 - David Seaman, Martin Keown, Ashley Cole and Ray Parlour*
139. *Old Trafford*
139. *1, in 1971*
140. *Huddersfield Town*

BOB WILSON

141. *1941*
142. *2*
143. *1963*
144. *John Radford*
145. *234*
146. *Wolverhampton Wanderers*
147. *European Fairs Cup (1970) and League Championship (1971)*
148. *Jim Furnell*
149. *All of them*
150. *The Willow Foundation*

DENNIS BERGKAMP

151. *1969*
152. *Inter Milan*
153. *Southampton, won 4-2 (home)*
154. *Middlesbrough (home)*
155. *Dutch*
156. *11*
157. *Leicester City*
158. *Bruce Rioch*

159.   Fear of flying
160.   Thierry Henry (2), Francis Jeffers

ARSENAL v. MANCHESTER UNITED

161.   Marc Overmars
162.   Eduardo Cesar Edu and Sylvain Wiltord
163.   0-1 (home)
164.   Alan Sunderland
165.   1-0 to Arsenal (home)
166.   Brian Talbot, Frank Stapleton and Alan Sunderland
167.   1989 (1989/90 season)
168.   Tony Adams, Nicolas Anelka, and Freddie Ljungberg
169.   The League Cup
170.   Alan Ball, John Radford and Ray Kennedy

ALAN SUNDERLAND

171.   1953
172.   Wolves
173.   Manchester United
174.   Terry Neill
175.   206: 204 (2)
176.   Tottenham Hotspur
177.   1980
178.   Ipswich Town
179.   Leeds United
180.   Norwich City

THIERRY HENRY

181.   1977
182.   Juventus
183.   1999
184.   2001/2002
185.   Bayern Munich, Lyon, Spartak Moscow and Valencia
186.   Leicester City, won 6-1 (December 2000)
187.   Liverpool 4-2 (home) and Leeds United 5-0 (home)
188.   West Ham United, won 3-1 (January 2003) and Roma, won 3-1 (November 2002)
189.   Tottenham Hotspur

190.   Ian Wright

LEAGUE CUP WINNERS - 1993
191.   Sheffield Wednesday
192.   2-1 to Arsenal
193.   Millwall and Crystal Palace
194.   Paul Merson and Steve Morrow
195.   Crystal Palace
196.   Nigel Winterburn
197.   Ian Wright
198.   Wembley Stadium
199.   David Seaman, David O'Leary, Nigel Winterburn, Steve Morrow,
        David Linighan, Tony Adams, Kevin Campbell, Ian Wright, Paul
        Davis, Paul Merson and Ray Parlour
200.   George Graham

PAT JENNINGS
201.   1945
202.   Tottenham Hotspur
203.   119
204.   237
205.   Keith Burkingshaw (Tottenham Hotspur)
206.   1987
207.   42 (all of them)
208.   John Lukic
209.   0
210.   FA Cup Winners medal - 1979

2002/2003
211.   2nd
212.   Birmingham City
213.   Sunderland
214.   1-0 to Arsenal
215.   PSV Eindhoven and Ajax
216.   West Ham United
217.   David Seaman, Rami Shaaban and Stuart Taylor
218.   Robert Pires and Jermaine Pennant
219.   78

220.   *Freddie Ljungberg*

ROBERT PIRES
221.   *1973*
222.   *Olympique Marseille*
223.   *Southampton, won 6-1 (May 2003)*
224.   *Bayern Leverkusen*
225.   *Football Writers' Player of the Year*
226.   *Southampton*
227.   *9*
228.   *Patrick Vieira*
229.   *Tottenham Hotspur*
230.   *Sunderland (19 August 2000)*

ALAN BALL
231.   *1971 (December)*
232.   *Everton*
233.   *Liverpool*
234.   *177*
235.   *45*
236.   *Bertie Mee*
237.   *Nottingham Forest (27 December 1971)*
238.   *72*
239.   *Southampton*
240.   *Blackpool*

PAUL MARINER
241.   *1953*
242.   *Ipswich Town*
243.   *Don Howe*
244.   *7*
245.   *14*
246.   *2*
247.   *35*
248.   *Portsmouth*
249.   *Stewart Robson*
250.   *Aston Villa*

MANAGER: ARSÈNE WENGER

251. 1949
252. 1996
253. Blackburn Rovers, October 1996 (away)
254. Nagoya Grampus Eight
255. Take charge of an English club
256. Premier League title (10 May 1998)
257. Nicolas Anelka
258. Monaco
259. Emmanuel Petit and Giles Grimandi
260. Patrick Vieira

EUROPEAN CUP WINNERS' CUP WINNERS - 1994

261. Parma
262. 1-0 to Arsenal
263. Alan Smith
264. Paris St. Germain
265. Odense
266. Alan Smith, Tony Adams, Ian Selley, Paul Merson, Kevin Campbell and Eddie McGoldrick
267. Torino
268. Eddie McGoldrick
269. David Seaman
270. George Graham

PETER STOREY

271. 1945
272. Leicester City
273. Billy Wright
274. Everton and Blackpool
275. 19
276. 9
277. John Radford
278. Stoke City
279. Gordon Banks
280. Fulham

RAY KENNEDY

281. 1969

282. Nottingham Forest
283. Tottenham Hotspur
284. Chelsea
285. 53
286. 19
287. Yeovil Town and Stoke City
288. St. Drammer, Grasshoppers Zurick and Ajax
289. Liverpool
290. 17

MALCOLM MACDONALD

291. 1950
292. Newcastle United
293. 42
294. 10
295. Bristol City
296. Norwich City
297. Birmingham City
298. Cyprus
299. 14
300. Fulham

JOHN RADFORD

301. 1947
302. Coventry City
303. 1965 (February)
304. 1973
305. 7 (between 1962 and 1976)
306. Tottenham Hotspur
307. 111
308. West Ham United
309. 2
310. Romania and Switzerland

LEAGUE CHAMPIONS - 1990/1991

311. 24
312. Steve Bould, Lee Dixon, David Seaman and Nigel Winterburn
313. Alan Smith

314. Paul Davis and Paul Merson
315. Crystal Palace
316. Alan Smith
317. 83 (should have had 85 but 2 were deducted)
318. Coventry City
319. 1
320. George Graham

PERRY GROVES

321. 1965
322. Watford, Southampton and Aston Villa
323. Wimbledon
324. Charlie Nicholas
325. 21
326. Everton
327. Colchester United
328. Vic Groves
329. George Graham
330. Southampton

TONY ADAMS

331. 1966
332. 5
333. 1987
334. Kenny Sansom
335. Sunderland
336. Tottenham Hotspur
337. 3
338. 1987
339. The League Cup and The FA Cup
340. Bobby Robson

MANAGER: DON HOWE

341. Terry Neill
342. 1983
343. Billy Wright
344. Liverpool
345. 1935

113

346. Tony Waiters
347. 1
348. 23
349. Queens Park Rangers
350. Right-back (defence)

PLAYERS NATONALITIES

351. Anders Limpar   Swedish
352. Nwankwo Kanu   Nigerian
353. Steve Morrow   Northern Irish
354. Tony Adams   English
355. Davor Suker   Croatian
356. Marc Overmars   Dutch
357. Robert Pires   French
358. Emmanuel Petit   French
359. John Jensen   Danish
360. Thierry Henry   French

ANDERS LIMPAR

361. FK Austria
362. Swedish
363. George Graham
364. Cremonese
365. 17
366. Liverpool (away) and Everton (home)
367. Everton
368. Liverpool
369. 11
370. 52

NIALL QUINN

371. Dublin
372. Liverpool
373. 8
374. Wimbledon and Manchester United
375. 14
376. Republic of Ireland
377. Huddersfield Town, Charlton Athletic and Tottenham Hotspur

378. Manchester City
379. Everton
380. Norwich City and Millwall

ASHLEY COLE
381. 1980
382. Crystal Palace
383. Middlesbrough (away)
384. Arsène Wenger
385. Cheryl Tweedy
386. Albania
387. Dynamo Kiev
388. Newcastle United
389. Sven Goran Eriksson
390. 3

ARSENAL v. CHELSEA
391. Sol Campbell and Sylvain Wiltord
392. Eduardo Cesar Edu
393. Ray Parlour and Freddie Ljungberg
394. Nwankwo Kanu
395. Dennis Bergkamp
396. 1992
397. UEFA Champions League
398. Sylvain Wiltord
399. David O'Leary, Alan Sunderland, Frank Stapleton (2) and David Price
400. Frank McLintock, John Radford and Ray Kennedy

LEAGUE POSITIONS - 2

401.	2000/2001	Premiership	2nd
402.	1995/1996	Premiership	5th
403.	1989/1990	Division One	4th
404.	1980/1981	Division One	3rd
405.	1975/1976	Division One	17th
406.	1970/1971	Division One	1st
407.	1966/1967	Division One	7th
408.	1960/1961	Division One	11th

| 409. | 1952/1953 | Division One | 1st |
| 410. | 1930/1931 | Division One | 1st |

DAVID ROCASTLE

411. **London**
412. **Michael Thomas and Alan Smith**
413. **Rocky**
414. **Chelsea and Aston Villa**
415. **24**
416. **14**
417. **Don Howe**
418. **Chelsea**
419. **Leeds United**
420. **Supporters' Player of the Year**

PAUL MERSON

421. **1968**
422. **Wimbledon, Queens Park Rangers and Norwich City**
423. **Middlesbrough**
424. **78**
425. **Crystal Palace**
426. **12**
427. **Merse**
428. **Brentford**
429. **1989**
430. **Manchester City (as substitute)**

SOL CAMPBELL

431. **1974**
432. **Middlesbrough (August 2001)**
433. **Tottenham Hotspur**
434. **Arsène Wenger**
435. **Sweden (2002)**
436. **2001 (July)**
437. **Aston Villa**
438. **The game was abandoned**
439. **Chelsea and Newcastle United**
440. **Premiership and FA Cup**

CHAMPIONS LEAGUE FINALISTS - 2006

441. Barcelona
442. 2-1 to Barcelona
443. Thierry Henry
444. Sol Campbell
445. Stade de France (Paris)
446. Jens Lehmann, Emmanuel Eboue, Kolo Toure, Sol Campbell, Ashley Cole, Robert Pires, Gilberto Silva, Francesc Fabregas, Aleksandr Hleb, Freddie Ljungberg and Thierry Henry
447. Manuel Almunia, Mathieu Flamini and Jose Antonio Reyes
448. Jens Lehmann
449. Samuel Eto'o and Juliano Belletti
450. Terje Hange

NICOLAS ANELKA

451. 1979
452. Paris St. Germain
453. Newcastle United
454. French
455. Leicester City (home)
456. Real Madrid
457. Shay Given (Newcastle United)
458. Chelsea
459. Paris St. Germain
460. Liverpool

STEVE BOULD

461. 1962
462. Wimbledon
463. Torquay United
464. 2
465. Stoke City
466. 1994 Cup Winners' Cup Final
467. Nottingham Forest and Newcastle United
468. 24
469. 3
470. Sunderland

WHERE DID THEY COME FROM?

471.	Tommy Docherty	Preston North End
472.	Chris Kiwomya	Ipswich Town
473.	Brian Marwood	Sheffield Wednesday
474.	Bobby Gould	Coventry City
475.	Steve Williams	Southampton
476.	Jeff Blockley	Coventry City
477.	Andy Linighan	Norwich City
478.	Brian Kidd	Manchester United
479.	Luis Boa Morte	Sporting Lisbon
480.	Ian Ure	Dundee

PATRICK VIEIRA

481. 1976
482. AC Milan
483. 1996
484. Senegal
485. Sheffield Wednesday
486. France
487. Emmanuel Petit
488. Arsène Wenger
489. 3
490. Juventus

LIAM BRADY

491. 1956
492. Malcolm MacDonald
493. Chippy
494. Leeds United
495. 43
496. Juventus, Sampdoria, Inter Milan and Ascoli
497. 72
498. Celtic
499. West Ham United
500. 13

FA CUP WINNERS - 1993

501. Sheffield Wednesday

502. *2-1 to Arsenal*
503. *Andy Linighan and Ian Wright*
504. *Tottenham Hotspur*
505. *Ian Wright*
506. *Ipswich Town*
507. *Yeovil Town*
508. *Leeds United*
509. *2 (against Ipswich Town and Tottenham Hotspur)*
510. *George Graham*

RAY PARLOUR

511. *1973*
512. *Liverpool (away)*
513. *The Romford Pele*
514. *5*
515. *Newcastle United*
516. *Chelsea*
517. *3*
518. *Sparta Prague and Valencia*
519. *10*
520. *Middlesbrough*

LEAGUE GOALSCORERS FOR ARSENAL - 1

521. *Jon Sammels*   *39*
522. *David O'Leary*   *11*
523. *Chris Kiwomya*   *3*
524. *Kevin Richardson*   *5*
525. *Derek Tapscott*   *62*
526. *Alan Smith*   *86*
527. *Gerry Ward*   *10*
528. *Anders Limpar*   *17*
529. *Tony Woodcock*   *56*
530. *George Graham*   *59*

TONY WOODCOCK

531. *Nottingham*
532. *FC Cologne*
533. *Nottingham Forest*

534. Aston Villa
535. 56
536. Northern Ireland (won 1-0)
537. 14
538. 42
539. FC Cologne
540. 16

2003/2004

541. 26
542. Liverpool and Leeds United
543. Jens Lehmann
544. Aston Villa
545. Leeds United
546. Everton (2-1), Middlesbrough (4-0), Aston Villa (2-0) and Manchester City (2-1)
547. 30
548. Eduardo Cesar Edu
549. Leicester City (home)
550. 0

CHARLIE NICHOLAS

551. 1961
552. Grimsby (away)
553. Terry Neill
554. Celtic
555. Liverpool
556. 20
557. 34
558. Wolverhampton Wanderers
559. Tottenham Hotspur
560. Aberdeen

LEAGUE APPEARANCES FOR ARSENAL

561. Brian Marwood   52
562. Brian Talbot   245 (9)
563. Neil Heaney   4 (3)
564. John Hartson   43 (10)

565.	Mark Flatts	9 (7)
566.	Kevin Campbell	124 (42)
567.	Alan Miller	6 (2)
568.	Pal Lydersen	12 (3)
569.	Paul Mariner	52 (8)
570.	Paul Shaw	1 (11)

PETER SIMPSON

571. Stan
572. Chelsea (home)
573. 10
574. European Fairs Club (1970), League Championship (1971) and FA Cup (1971)
575. 1945
576. Ipswich Town
577. 1969
578. Billy Wright, Bertie Mee and Terry Neill
579. Wolverhampton Wanderers
580. John Radford and Ray Kennedy

ARSENAL v. TOTTENHAM HOTSPUR

581. 2-1 (2-1 and 2-1: 4-2 on aggregate)
582. Michael Thomas
583. Nigel Winterburn, Brian Marwood and Alan Smith
584. David O'Leary (1973-1993)
585. Joe Hulme
586. 1990 (13 October)
587. 1-0 to Tottenham Hotspur (at White Hart Lane)
588. 1980 (7 April)
589. 2-0
590. Pat Jennings

CHARLIE GEORGE

591. 1950
592. Derby County
593. 31
594. Joe Corrigan
595. Ray Clemence (Liverpool)

596. *Portsmouth, Manchester City and Leicester City*
597. *Derby County*
598. *1*
599. *Bertie Mee*
600. *Tottenham Hotspur*

VIV ANDERSON

601. *1956*
602. *Tottenham Hotspur*
603. *Win a full England cap*
604. *9*
605. *Czechoslovakia*
606. *30*
607. *Aston Villa and Chelsea*
608. *Turkey (1984) and Yugoslavia (1986)*
609. *Chelsea (1-1 draw)*
610. *Barnsley*

LEAGUE APPEARANCES FOR ARSENAL

611.	Liam Brady	*227 (8)*
612.	Andy Cole	*0 (1)*
613.	Frank McLintock	*312 (2)*
614.	Pat Jennings	*237*
615.	Paul Davis	*331 (20)*
616.	Bob Wilson	*234*
617.	Paul Merson	*289 (38)*
618.	David O'Leary	*523 (35)*
619.	Frank Stapleton	*223 (2)*
620.	Kenny Sansom	*314*

DAVID PLATT

621. *1966*
622. *Sampdoria*
623. *1-1*
624. *Everton*
625. *62*
626. *27*
627. *Aston Villa*

628.   Patrick Vieira and Nicolas Anelka
629.   Bari, Juventus and Sampdoria
630.   Barnsley, Manchester United and Leicester City

LEAGUE CHAMPIONS - 1970/1971

631.   29
632.   Ray Kennedy
633.   65
634.   16
635.   Bertie Mee
636.   Bob Wilson, George Armstrong and Frank McLintock
637.   Manchester United, Nottingham Forest and Everton
638.   Ray Kennedy
639.   Ipswich Town (1-0 away and 3-2 home)
640.   Tottenham Hotspur

PAUL DAVIS

641.   London
642.   West Bromwich Albion
643.   Charlton Athletic (March 1989)
644.   Brentford
645.   Nottingham Forest
646.   1995
647.   The FA Cup and The League Cup
648.   11
649.   Leicester City
650.   Terry Neill

LEE DIXON

651.   Manchester
652.   Stoke City
653.   22
654.   George Graham
655.   Luton Town
656.   Bury
657.   Norwich City, Queens Park Rangers and Southampton
658.   Czechoslovakia
659.   Bobby Robson

660.   4

THE CHAMPIONS LEAGUE
661.   Chelsea
662.   7
663.   Wembley Stadium
664.   Barcelona
665.   PSV Eindhoven
666.   Jens Lehmann
667.   Valencia
668.   Freddie Ljungberg, Eduardo Cesar Edu, Robert Pires and Thierry Henry (2)
669.   David Seaman, John Lukic, Stuart Taylor and Alex Manninger
670.   Roma

EMMANUEL PETIT
671.   1970
672.   Monaco
673.   Wimbledon (5-0 at home)
674.   French
675.   Leeds United
676.   1998
677.   Nicolas Anelka and Nwankwo Kanu
678.   Marc Overmars
679.   Preston North End (won 4-2 away)
680.   Chelsea

LEAGUE POSITIONS - 3
681.	2002/2003	Premiership	2nd
682.	1997/1998	Premiership	1st
683.	1993/1994	Premiership	4th
684.	1983/1984	Division One	6th
685.	1976/1977	Division One	8th
686.	1968/1969	Division One	4th
687.	1955/1956	Division One	5th
688.	1919/1920	Division One	10th
689.	1913/1914	Division Two	3rd
690.	1900/1901	Division Two	7th

WILLIE YOUNG

691. Edinburgh
692. Tottenham Hotspur
693. Terry Neill
694. 11
695. Centre back
696. Norwich City
697. Malcolm MacDonald
698. Wrexham
699. Nottingham Forest
700. Southampton (away), Derby County (home)
     and Bolton Wanderers (home)

ARSENAL HISTORY - 1

701. 3
702. Patrick Vieira
703. 1971 and 2004
704. Rotherham
705. Tony Adams
706. Leicester Fosse
707. Olof Mellberg (Aston Villa)
708. Wembley Stadium
709. Sunderland
710. 55

JOHN JENSEN

711. 1965
712. Danish
713. Queens Park Rangers
714. 1
715. Norwich City (home), lost 4-2
716. 32
717. 93 (5) = 98
718. George Graham
719. The FA Cup (both the Final and Final replay)
720. Brondby (Denmark)

MARC OVERMARS

721. 1973
722. Ajax
723. Middlesbrough (home)
724. Arsène Wenger
725. Newcastle United
726. 12
727. Go Ahead Eagles, Willem II and Ajax
728. 3-0 to Arsenal
729. Leeds United
730. West Ham United

2005/2006

731. Newcastle United
732. Jens Lehmann
733. Pascal Cygan and Thierry Henry
734. Robert Pires
735. 27
736. Real Madrid
737. 4th
738. 20
739. Thierry Henry (3), Philippe Senderos, Robert Pires, Gilberto Silva and Aleksandr Hleb
740. Wigan Athletic

GRAHAM RIX

741. 1957
742. 7
743. 17
744. 41
745. 1974
746. Portsmouth
747. Ron Greenwood
748. Brentford
749. SM Caen and Le Havre
750. Hearts

ARSENAL v. WEST HAM UNITED

751. 0-0 (away)
752. Brian Kidd
753. Ian Wright
754. Marc Overmars (2), Ian Wright and Dennis Bergkamp
755. Marc Overmars and Ian Wright
756. John Hartson and Dennis Bergkamp
757. Trevor Brooking
758. 2-0 to Arsenal
759. Brian Talbot, Paul Mariner and Tony Woodcock
760. John Hartson

LEAGUE GOALSCORERS FOR ARSENAL - 2

761.	Liam Brady	43
762.	Charlie George	31
763.	David Rocastle	24
764.	Steve Walford	3
765.	Alan Sunderland	55
766.	Paul Dickov	3
767.	Graham Rix	41
768.	Willie Young	11
769.	Andy Linighan	5
770.	Peter Goring	51

FA CUP WINNERS - 1979

771. Manchester United
772. 3-2 to Arsenal
773. Brian Talbot, Alan Sunderland and Frank Stapleton
774. 4
775. Villa Park, Aston Villa
776. Southampton
777. Pat Jennings
778. Frank Stapleton
779. Wembley Stadium
780. Terry Neill

FRANK STAPLETON

781. 1956

782. Sheffield Wednesday, Sheffield Wednesday, Nottingham Forest, Wolverhampton Wanderers, Manchester United
783. Tottenham Hotspur
784. Ajax
785. 75
786. Manchester United
787. David Price
788. 70
789. Ipswich Town (home)
790. Bradford City

GEORGE ARMSTRONG
791. 1944
792. Blackpool
793. Electrician
794. Geordie
795. 53
796. 1970
797. Tottenham Hotspur
798. 500
799. 1963 (February)
800. Leicester City

FA CUP WINNERS - 1971
801. Liverpool
802. 2-1 to Arsenal
803. Charlie George and Eddie Kelly
804. Stoke City
805. Bob Wilson
806. 5
807. Yeovil Town
808. Yeovil Town (3rd round), Portsmouth (4th round), Manchester City (5th round), Leicester City (Quarter-Final) and Stoke City (Semi Final)
809. Ray Clemence
810. Bertie Mee

1992/1993 - FIRST PREMIER LEAGUE SEASON

811.   10th
812.   Norwich City
813.   4-2 to Norwich City
814.   Coventry City (home) and Crystal Palace (home)
815.   David Seaman and Alan Miller
816.   40
817.   15
818.   Paul Merson
819.   George Graham
820.   15

FREDDIE LJUNGBERG

821.   1977
822.   Manchester United
823.   Swedish
824.   1998 (September)
825.   10
826.   8
827.   BK Halmstad
828.   6
829.   Arsène Wenger
830.   USA

LEAGUE CHAMPIONS - 2001/2002

831.   26
832.   24
833.   Freddie Ljungberg
834.   Middlesbrough
835.   Aston Villa (in a 2-1 win)
836.   Leicester City
837.   4-0 to Arsenal
838.   Leeds United (2-1), Newcastle United (3-1) and Charlton Athletic (4-2)
839.   Chelsea and Newcastle United
840.   Everton

KEVIN CAMPBELL

841.   1970
842.   94
843.   Leyton Orient and Leicester City
844.   George Graham
845.   46
846.   Ipswich Town
847.   Paris St. Germain
848.   4-0 to Arsenal
849.   Norwich City, Coventry City, Coventry City and Crystal Palace
850.   Nottingham Forest

LEAGUE GOALSCORERS FOR ARSENAL - 3

851.   Ian Wright   128
852.   Joe Hulme   107
853.   Alan Smith   86
854.   Reg Lewis   103
855.   Jimmy Brain   125
856.   Joe Baker   93
857.   Ted Drake   124
858.   Jack Lambert   98
859.   Frank Stapleton   75
860.   Cliff Bastin   150

DAVID PRICE

861.   1955
862.   Liverpool
863.   Stoke City
864.   Terry Neill
865.   16
866.   Peterborough United
867.   1
868.   Crystal Palace
869.   David O'Leary and Graham Rix
870.   Leyton Orient

SAMMY NELSON

871.   1949

872. Ipswich Town
873. Norwich City, Birmingham City and Aston Villa
874. Leeds United
875. Frank Stapleton
876. 10
877. 1979 (against Manchester United, 3-2)
878. 51
879. Brighton & Hove Albion
880. Brighton & Hove Albion

LEAGUE CHAMPIONS - 1997/1998

881. 23
882. Manchester United
883. Dennis Bergkamp
884. Barnsley and Wimbledon
885. Dennis Bergkamp
886. Marc Overmars
887. 2 (2 draws - 0-0, 1-1)
888. David Seaman and Alex Manninger
889. Arsène Wenger
890. Liverpool (4-0) and Aston Villa (1-0)

KENNY SANSOM

891. 1958
892. Crystal Palace
893. Clive Allen and Paul Barron
894. 86
895. Wales
896. Norman (after Norman Wisdom)
897. 1981
898. 6
899. 2-0 to Arsenal
900. West Ham United

NIGEL WINTERBURN

901. 1963
902. Wimbledon
903. Italy

904. 2
905. Tottenham Hotspur, Norwich City and Wimbledon
906. Psycho Squirrel
907. Southampton
908. Everton
909. 2-0 to Arsenal
910. West Ham United

MANAGER: TERRY NEILL
911. 1942
912. 20 years old
913. Tottenham Hotspur
914. Pat Jennings
915. Pat Rice
916. 59
917. Bertie Mee
918. Crystal Palace
919. Hull City
920. Brian Talbot

MARTIN KEOWN
921. 1966
922. France
923. 43
924. Everton
925. He was cup-tied
926. Nottingham Forest (away)
927. Graham Taylor
928. Arsenal
929. Leicester City
930. Nottingham Forest

LEAGUE CHAMPIONS - 1988/1989
931. 22
932. John Lukic, David Rocastle and Nigel Winterburn
933. Wimbledon
934. 24
935. 17

936. Norwich City (home)
937. Nigel Winterburn, Alan Smith and Brian Marwood
938. Derby County
939. Liverpool
940. Alan Smith and Michael Thomas

MANAGER: BRUCE RIOCH

941. 1995
942. George Graham
943. Bolton Wanderers
944. David Platt
945. Dennis Bergkamp
946. John Lukic
947. 5th
948. Torquay United
949. Scotland
950. Aston Villa

ALAN SMITH

951. 1962
952. 13
953. Leicester City
954. 2: 1988/1989 and 1990/1991
955. Parma
956. Manchester United (home)
957. FK Austria
958. Portsmouth
959. Chelsea, Newcastle United and Swindon Town
960. Wimbledon

ARSENAL - HISTORY - 2

961. Herbert Chapman
962. Tom Parker
963. Gilberto Silva
964. Stewart Robson (17 years, 57 days) v. Tottenham Hotspur in 1982
965. John Lukic (39 years, 336 days) v. Derby County in 2000
966. 20
967. Loughborough Town

968.   Score in every Premier League game
969.   Robin Van Persie
970.   38,419

FA CUP WINNERS - 2002

971.   Chelsea
972.   2-0 to Arsenal
973.   Ray Parlour and Freddie Ljungberg
974.   David Seaman
975.   Eduardo Cesar Edu, Nwankwo Kanu, Martin Keown, Thierry Henry and Sylvain Wiltord
976.   Freddie Ljungberg, Thierry Henry, Nwankwo Kanu and Dennis Bergkamp
977.   Middlesbrough
978.   Liverpool
979.   Sol Campbell, Robert Pires and Dennis Bergkamp
980.   5-2 to Arsenal

BOB McNAB

981.   1943
982.   Huddersfield Town
983.   Liverpool
984.   4
985.   Romania
986.   4
987.   Left back (defence)
988.   Wolverhampton Wanderers
989.   6 (4 League and 2 League Cup)
990.   Norwich City

FA CUP WINNERS - 1998

991.   Newcastle United
992.   2-0 to Arsenal
993.   Marc Overmars and Dennis Bergkamp
994.   Wembley Stadium
995.   Wolverhampton Wanderers
996.   Crystal Palace and West Ham United
997.   Tony Adams

special days for seriously ill young adults

ABOUT
WILLOW FOUNDATION

Special days aim to provide young adults living with life-threatening conditions a chance to escape the pressures of their daily routine and share quality time with family and/or friends.

Every special day is of the young person's choosing - it could involve fulfilling a lifelong dream or it could simply offer an opportunity to bring some much needed normality back into their lives.

The Foundation will endeavour to fulfil the special day request however imaginative and, if possible, exceed expectations.

To date the charity has organised and funded special days for young adults living with a wide range of serious conditions including amongst others; cancer, motor neurone disease, cystic fibrosis, organ failure, multiple sclerosis (later stages) and heart disease.

Bob & Megs Wilson founded the Willow Foundation in memory of their daughter, Anna who died of cancer aged 31.

For more information please contact:
Willow Foundation, Willow House, 18 Salisbury Square,
Hatfield, Hertfordshire, AL9 5BE
Tel: 01707 259777   Fax: 01707 259289
or email: info@willowfoundation.org.uk

REVIEWS

"Reckon you're a true Arsenal fan? From Plumstead Common to the Emirates Stadium, from Sam Hollis to Arsene Wenger - it's all in the with The Gooners Quiz Book!" - www.4thegame.com

"A great idea for quizzes after the match, in the pub, or keep it to yourself and amaze your mates with your knowledge of a 100 years of Arsenal History." - www.arsenaltimes.com

"A must for all Arsenal fans from all generations."
www.arsenalscotland.com

"The "Gooners Quiz Book" is a great source of fun and information for any true Arsenal supporter. No self-respecting Gooner should be without a copy. If you don't gain hours of enjoyment from this book, you're probably a Spurs' fan." - Mark Barbeau, Arsenal America (San Francisco) Supporters Club (Manager)

"This book makes you put your thinking cap on! The questions certainly brought back some good memories. I also learnt alot of things that I didnt know - well done Chris." - Niel Neophytou, Arsenal Cyprus Supporters Club (Secretary)

"Never before have Gooners had such a miscellany of questions posed to test their Arsenal knowledge. If you didn't know the club's history before, you will after you tackle 'The Gooners Quiz Book'."
- Doug Goodwin, Arsenal America (Atlanta) Supporters Club